Policy Studies in Employment and Welfare Number 24

General Editor: Sar A. Levitan

Labor Issues of American International Trade and Investment

Daniel J.B. Mitchell

The Johns Hopkins University Press, Baltimore and London

The National Manpower Policy Task Force is a private nonprofit organization of academicians who have a special interest and expertise in the area of manpower. The Task Force is primarily concerned with furthering research on manpower problems and assessing related policy issues. It sponsors three types of publications:

1. Policy Statements in which the Task Force members are actively involved as coauthors.
2. Studies commissioned by the Task Force and reviewed by a committee prior to publication.
3. Studies prepared by members of the Task Force, but not necessarily reviewed by other members.

Publications under Nos. 2 and 3 above do not necessarily represent the views of the Task Force or its members except those whose names appear on the study.

This study was prepared under a contract to the Task Force from the Office of Research and Development, Manpower Administration, U.S. Dept. of Labor.

Contents

List of Tables

Preface

This study is designed to familiarize the manpower specialist with the interrelation between international trade and investment and the labor market. The reader is assumed to have no special background in international economics. As might be expected, the tools of international economic analysis are simply extrapolations of the techniques used in "domestic economics." And as is sometimes true in other areas of economics, these tools sometimes suggest that what may appear to be the obvious answer to a question is not necessarily the correct answer.

The temptation in writing a manpower-oriented book on labor and international trade problems is to concentrate on the one manpower program in the area: adjustment assistance for import-injured workers. Two chapters have been devoted to that program. But the story of adjustment assistance has been a sad tale of a limited program of uncertain objectives and without a solid constituency. Two major investigations of adjustment assistance have been undertaken previously by other researchers. A third will be forthcoming shortly.[1] Hence, it seemed important for this study to encompass a wider scope.

Chapter 1 covers two major topics. The first is a very brief survey of American international trade and trade policy, not specifically oriented to labor issues, but strictly a review. The interested reader without a background may wish to pursue these subjects further in other studies. Chapter 1 also includes a review of what international economic analysis has to say about the labor market. The emphasis is on income distribution, real wages, employment, and unemployment.

One important factor relating international trade to the labor market is the "labor-intensity" of imports relative to exports. Chapter 1 explains the background of this concept, while Chapter 2 provides an empirical review. The finding of Chapter 2 that imports were becoming labor-intensive relative to exports in recent years will be greeted with mixed reactions. Some will be disquieted by the possible long-term implications of the development for labor; others will downplay its significance and call for more data. In any case, it is a development of interest to those concerned with long-range manpower trends.

As already noted, Chapters 3 and 4 are devoted to the development of the worker adjustment assistance program. This program was originally established by the Trade Expansion Act of 1962 and was extended and enlarged by the Trade Act of 1974. Chapter 3 reviews its history. Discussion of the 1974 revisions is found in Chapter 4.

Chapter 5 summarizes what is known about multinational corporations and their impact on labor. It is an apologetic chapter for two reasons. First, little is known about the effects of such corporations on labor. The main problem in analyzing multinationals is that their functions—such as the transfer of goods and financial capital from one country to another—can be and often are also carried out through other institutional arrangements. The key question revolves around the *independent* effect of the multinationals, which is hard to determine. In addition, multinational corporations raise many questions outside the labor arena. Chapter 5, therefore, is forced to take a one-sided view of a multifaceted issue.

The writing of this study was both helped and hindered by the currency of its subject matter. On one hand, the currency was helpful because of the considerable body of recent literature. But timeliness has its drawbacks. While much of this study was written, the Trade Act of 1974 was making its way through Congress. Congressional prerogatives of amendments were exercised continuously, making it difficult for the author to keep up and necessitating rewriting at times. Moreover, it was not clear until the final days of the 1974 session that the bill would be passed. Chapters 3 and 4 could not be written until passage was assured.

The new bill created two minor problems of nomenclature. One section changed the name of the Tariff Commission to the International Trade Commission. This posed a problem—particularly in Chapter 3—since the Tariff Commission was involved in the worker adjustment assistance program up until the bill was passed. To avoid confusion, the name "Tariff Commission" is generally used in the text to describe the agency. In addition, at the last moment, the name of the bill was changed from the Trade *Reform* Act of 1974 to the Trade Act of 1974. The reader should not be confused if he or she comes across documents that refer to the former name. The two acts are one and the same.

A number of people assisted in the preparation of this study. At the Department of Labor, Monroe Dowling, Marvin Fooks, Harry Grubert, and Dominic Sorrentino were especially helpful, as were Kenneth Mason and Charles Ervin at the Tariff Commission. I also benefited from conversations with a number of California state and federal officials. Robert Goldstone handled the computer operations underlying Chapter 2 and was of great assistance in locating important source material. The Institute of Industrial Relations, UCLA, assisted by providing Mr. Goldstone's services and giving me additional research time. Elizabeth Jager of the AFL–CIO was kind enough to provide a number of helpful documents. Robert Baldwin of the University of Wisconsin-Madison also directed me to some important sources of information.

A reading committee of Gerald Somers and Ray Marshall made helpful suggestions on an earlier version of this study. Robert Taggart also provided useful input. Editorial suggestions that improved readability and brought the study down to manageable dimensions were made by Henry Y. K. Tom of The Johns Hopkins University Press. A special note of appreciation goes to my wife, Alice, who let me get away with going to Washington during the holiday season to gather data.

Finally, I wish to thank Sar Levitan and the members of the National Manpower Policy Task Force for sponsoring my efforts.

Los Angeles   D. J. B. M.

Labor Issues
of American International
Trade and Investment

1

Background on the Trade-Labor Issue

Background on U.S. Foreign Trade

Manpower problems and international economics sometimes are clearly related. International economics, however, is not likely to be part of the standard "tool kit" of the manpower specialist. This chapter is in no sense a primer on the international sector, but seeks to provide a general background on foreign trade, particularly as it relates to American labor. Certain aspects of international investment that can be separated at this stage are discussed in Chapter 5.

Exports and imports traditionally are divided into goods and services. United States trade in goods is highly diversified, running from crude materials to sophisticated finished goods. Trade in services also covers a wide range, including insurance, tourist facilities, and airline seats, along with the "services" of capital which are recognized in the form of international transactions involving dividends, interest, and royalties.

By some measures, foreign trade is not very important to the United States. In 1974, exports of goods and services came to only 10 percent of the U.S. GNP. Imports came to only 9.9 percent. These ratios have drifted upward during the period following World War II. The small absolute figures seem to suggest a lack of significance, particularly when compared to a country like Holland where the ratios are roughly 50 percent.

1

Aggregate figures, of course, do not tell the whole story. Virtually all U.S. consumption of some products is imported, such as coffee, bananas, rubber, and diamonds. Few exporters are totally dependent on foreign customers. But over one-fifth of U.S. goods exported in 1970 came from "four-digit" industries that sold at least one-quarter of their output abroad. [1]

In any case, dependency ratios are misleading. Even where the trade proportion is small, the existence of a world market for a good links its domestic price to the world price. In turn, these foreign-origin prices affect the prices for other products which are substitutes or are made from foreign-traded inputs. World inflation can be translated quickly into American inflation through these channels.

Over two-thirds of U.S. commodity exports and imports go to, or come from, other industrialized western countries. Proximity plays a role, too. In 1974, over 21 percent of U.S. goods exported and imported involved Canada. Trade with Canada has been boosted since 1965 by a special agreement permitting free trade in new cars and parts, thus integrating the North American auto industry.

A wide range of government programs influence trade flows. On the export side, for example, sales are promoted through low-interest loans by the Export-Import Bank. Various promotional activities abroad are underwritten by the U.S. government. Exports of certain products, however, have been limited or embargoed for reasons of international politics and national security.

Imports are restricted through a variety of tariff and nontariff policies. The tariff issue has played a major role in American history. Conflict between the export-oriented South and the protection-oriented North is considered a major cause of the Civil War. After the Civil War, Democratic administrations typically lowered tariffs and Republicans raised them. These undulations culminated in the extremely high Smoot-Hawley Tariff of 1930. Tariff history since that time has consisted of the efforts of both Democratic and Republican presidents to scale down the Smoot-Hawley rates.

During the 1930s, the Roosevelt administrations embarked on a series of international negotiations aimed at achieving reciprocal tariff reductions. Nations that cooperated received the benefit of "most-favored nation" tariff rates on their products. After World War II, the United States was one of the signatories to GATT, the General Agreement on Trade and Tariffs, which has provided the vehicle for subsequent trade negotiations. However, Congress refused to go along with a proposal to establish an international agency to supervise world trade.

Formation of two major trade blocs in Europe in the late 1950s created pressure in the United States for expanded trade negotiations, as exporters feared they would lose ground in the profitable European market. Six countries—France, West Germany, Italy, Belgium, Luxemburg, and Holland—formed the European Economic Community (EEC) or Common Market. Seven other countries, including Britain, formed the European Free Trade Association (EFTA). In both blocs, relatively free trade between member states was permitted, thus putting outsiders at a disadvantage.

The American response was the Trade Expansion Act of 1962 (TEA), which authorized the "Kennedy Round" tariff-reduction negotiations. TEA repealed a provision in U.S. tariff laws allowing semiautomatic tariff increases if the U.S. Tariff Commission found that a domestic industry was injured by imports. A much more limited mechanism was provided, which made it more difficult for domestic interests to obtain such protection and safeguarded the Kennedy Round concessions. In addition, TEA established a program granting financial aid to workers and firms injured by import concessions.

Organized labor generally supported TEA when it was passed. But by the time the Kennedy Round tariff cuts began to go into effect in the late 1960s, labor's attitude had changed dramatically. Demands were made for the passage of the Burke-Hartke bill to allow import quotas. Despite this domestic pressure, other new forces had begun to push for further trade liberalization. Especially significant was the rise of U.S.-based multinational firms that saw their interests tied to expanded trade and feared the "trade wars" and foreign political repercussions of a restrictive U.S. import policy.

Just as they had earlier, European developments also played an important role. Britain joined the Common Market in 1973, bringing in other nations. The EEC now had a population size comparable to that of the United States. Effectively, it was even bigger, since several nonmember countries negotiated special trade agreements with the enlarged Common Market. American export interests became concerned over the loss of potential sales to inside suppliers.

The balance of political forces ultimately led to the passage of the Trade Act of 1974 (TA). Under TA, new negotiating authority was provided to the president. As part of the policy of detente, the granting of most-favored nation treatment for imports from the Soviet Union was permitted, conditional on a less restrictive (Jewish) emigration policy on the part of the Russians. (This program was stillborn when the Soviets rejected the emigration proviso.) An expanded program of adjustment assistance was created for workers, firms, and communities injured by imports, this time intended more to mute labor opposition to the bill than to win support.

Economic Analysis of Trade

A reading of U.S. tariff history suggests that "political" forces and sectoral interests have dominated the fashioning of U.S. trade policy. The viewpoint of academic economists traditionally has been that international trade is a good thing and that restrictions are to be avoided. Despite recognition that trade policy is not determined through dispassionate analysis of economic writings, the implications of the international economic literature must be explored. Can the views of academic economists be squared with the fears expressed by organized labor that trade is now having an adverse effect? Are there new factors that "have made the old 'free trade' concepts and their 'protectionist' opposites outdated and increasingly irrelevant"?[2]

As the reader might expect, much depends on underlying assumptions. Equally important is the matter of perspective.

The benefits from trade can be viewed at different levels. For convenience, these levels may be described as the world view, the national view, the class view, and the sectoral view. These four perspectives help to illuminate much that has been written about the trade issue.

The World View

In much of the international economic literature, the world is viewed as made up of countries whose behavior is similar to that of individuals with goods to trade. Textbook economic analysis at the domestic level tends to suggest a presumption for a laissez-faire policy of competition and free trade, so it is not surprising that the international equivalent ends up in much the same place.

Of course, international economists recognize that the behavior of a country with many diverse elements is not the same as the behavior of individuals and that the other assumptions of international economic analysis are highly simplified. But the prevailing view is summed up by one major textbook: "The presumption lies in favor of freer trade, even though not all steps toward freer trade are desirable. . . . Free trade should be likened to honesty which is the best policy, as is well known. . . but it must be held in check on limited occasions."[3] In both the domestic and international settings an individual (country) might gain at the expense of his fellows through the exercise of monopoly or monopsony power. But one man's gain is another's loss, and the gain usually entails an inefficiency of production and consumption. Hence, from the world view, everyone would be better off in some aggregate sense by refraining from interference with trade.

The National View

Although economists tend to take the world view, the early development of thought on the foreign trade question looked at the issue from the viewpoint of a particular nation. In 1817, David Ricardo, the famous British political economist, asked himself if it could be shown that a nation would be better off as the result of an opportunity to trade.[4] He developed the theory of "comparative advantage" that suggested that a nation would always benefit by exporting products it produced relatively efficiently and by importing in exchange products in which it was relatively inefficient in production.

There was a natural tendency, at first, to confuse "trade" with "free trade." Later it was recognized that a country that was a dominant seller or a dominant buyer could follow restrictive policies which exploited this characteristic to its own benefit. In recent years, the most vivid example of the use of such power has been the cartel of oil-exporting countries. By coordinating their pricing policies, the oil nations have greatly increased their revenues at the expense of oil consumers. The price is kept high through restrictions on output, which create an inefficient and artificial energy shortage.

Of course, even if a country does have monopoly or monopsony power, it may suffer from repercussions if it uses export or import tariffs to benefit itself at the expense of others. Economic or even military retaliation is a possibility. Trade wars, in which countries impose tariffs in response to other countries' tariffs, can quickly eliminate the initial gains.

The Class View

Just as the world view ignores questions of income distribution between countries, the national view obscures questions of income distribution between economic classes. But unless such questions are considered, it is impossible to consider the impact of trade on labor.

The literature on international trade tends to consider labor and capital as factors of production rather than as social classes. There is, of course, a distinction. Individuals who are employees may nevertheless receive some returns from capital. Many blue-collar workers, for example, are involved in pension or insurance programs that draw income from investments, or they may receive interest on savings deposits. Despite these qualifications, however, there is no harm in associating the factor labor with the class labor, since wealth definitely is concentrated.

Explicit treatment of factors of production began as an effort to interpret comparative advantage. As noted earlier, the notion of relative efficiency or inefficiency in production was used to explain trade patterns beginning in the early nineteenth century. Not until the early twentieth century, however, was explanation for these efficiencies and inefficiencies based on factor supplies. In the simplest terms, the explanation was that countries with large supplies of capital relative to labor would export capital-intensive products (products that used much capital relative to labor in production) and would import labor-intensive products. Countries with much labor relative to capital—less-developed countries—would export labor-intensive products and import capital-intensive products.

The factor-supply explanation had an interesting income corollary. A labor-abundant, less-developed country would find that its labor-intensive industries were stimulated by trade, since their output would be needed for export. Expansion of these industries would absorb more capital than labor, thus bidding up the price of labor. Real wages would tend to rise as a result of trade. Of course, the reverse tendency would occur in the developed world. Labor-intensive industries would be depressed. Thus, downward pressure on real wages would result in industrialized countries. Labor would be hurt by trade, and capital would be benefited.

The conclusion of the factor-supply explanation is interesting, since it suggests that trade and immigration are at least somewhat interchangeable. If free immigration were allowed, workers would tend to move from low-wage, less-developed countries to high-wage industrial areas. This would tend to raise wages where they came from and lower them where they went. In essence, the factor-supply explanation said that it did not matter very much in terms of the wage effect whether people moved to the factories, or the factories moved to the people.

Inadvertently, the factor-supply explanation of trade patterns suggested a possible rationale for protection from the viewpoint of labor in developed countries. The explanation suggested that trade had a wage-depressing effect. Presumably, therefore, barriers to trade such as tariffs or quotas would push in the

7

opposite direction and tend to raise real wages.[5] Of course, the importance of this effect would be small in a country such as the U.S. where the trade sector is relatively small compared with overall economic activity.

After World War II, the greater availability of economic data and the beginnings of the computer age made possible empirical investigation of the factor-supply explanation. An early test by Wassily Leontief based on 1947 data produced startling results. He found that the capital-to-labor ratio—dollar value of capital stock divided by man-years—was higher in imports than in exports, $18,184 versus $13,991.[6] That is, in contradiction to the factor-supply explanation, the capital-rich U.S. economy imported capital-intensive products rather than exporting them!

Almost as soon as these results were out, new explanations were developed. Some argued that the word *capital* should include human capital, the value of education and training embodied in the work force. Empirical investigations revealed that U.S. exports seem to embody a greater level of worker skill than do imports. For example, table 1.1 shows the result of a study of labor content of American tade as of the early 1960s. If the work force used to produce exports is compared with the

Table 1.1. Educational Attainment of the Labor Force in U.S. Exports and Competitive Imports*

Occupations with median educational attainment of	Exports	Imports
5–8 years	23.0	27.5
9–11 years	42.9	42.9
12 years	29.8	25.8
13–15 years	2.2	1.9
16 or more years	2.1	1.9
Total	100.0	100.0

SOURCE: Daniel J. B. Mitchell, "The Occupational Structure of U.S. Exports and Imports," *Quarterly Review of Economics and Business,* 10 (Winter 1970): 22, 26.

*Percent in export or competitive import labor forces by median education level of occupational class. Includes secondary labor requirements of industries that supply export or import-competing industries.

work force that would have been used to produce the imports, the occupations involved in exports tend to be composed of slightly more-educated workers.

In recent years the Leontief paradox seems to have eroded. U.S. imports have tended to become more labor-intensive as the original factor-supply explanation suggested. This turn of events might be due in part to such forces as the final recovery from the effects of the war, the reduction in trade barriers during the Kennedy Round, or perhaps, the greater similarity in education and technology among the major trading nations. Whatever the cause, the change suggests that the income corollary of the factor-supply explanation—the topic of Chapter 2—bears examination.

The Sectoral View

The class view of trade emphasizes opposed economic interests of capital and labor. But, in the short run, at the micro level, these interests may run in the same direction. An increase in protection of an industry permits an increase in price and production. Consumers may be unhappy with the price impact, but the industry's owners clearly will benefit, and some of the gain may be captured by labor, particularly if it has a union with bargaining strength.

Protection for an industry may take different forms. A tariff is simply a tax levied on imports of the product. If the world price of an item is $100, and a tax of $25 is imposed, then the domestic price can rise to $125 before foreigners can compete in the marketplace. On the other hand, the tariff method does place some limitations on domestic producers, since if they raise their price above the sum of the world price and tariff, they will lose sales to foreign suppliers.

In contrast, a quota system can be less limiting to prices. A quota is simply a quantitative limit on the volume of a product that may be imported. Once the import quota has been sold, domestic interests have the marketplace to themselves. Both sectoral capital and labor interests have economic reasons to prefer quotas. More recently a political motivation has been introduced. In some industries such as steel, apparel, and textiles, industry interests have pressed the U.S. government to persuade foreign suppliers "voluntarily" to limit their sales in the American market, a sort of informal quota.[7] Informal quotas avoid some of the pitfalls of seeking aid from Congress or the Tariff Commission (now the International Trade Commission).

The Employment Impact of Trade

So far, the discussion has centered on the real income effects of trade. From the national or sectoral viewpoints, trade has the effect of reallocating the pattern of production and therefore of employment. To the extent that trade encourages national specialization, its net result is to encourage particular types of employment and production in some countries and to discourage them in others. Within a country at the sectoral level, foreign trade makes some industries expand while others contract.

The issue of employment patterns has been raised in recent statements by spokesmen for organized labor fearing the specter of a nation of "hamburger stands" with no heavy industry.[8] Presumably, in this nightmare vision, the United States will export mainly agricultural commodities which are capital-intensive and dependent on natural resources. It will live off dividends from foreign investments and will import much of its consumption requirements for manufactures. Domestic employment will be concentrated in services and distribution.

The United States has moved in the direction of a service and distribution economy since World War II. Manufacturing, mining, and construction jobs accounted for 42 percent of non-farm employment in 1948, but only 31 percent in 1974. Of course, part of the reason for this shift has been the more rapid rate of productivity growth in these "traditional" sectors. Construction productivity is notoriously difficult to measure. However, manufacturing productivity rose at an annual rate of 3 percent from 1950 to 1973. In contrast, total private nonfarm productivity has risen at only a 2.6 percent rate. Spotty data on the government sector suggests a productivity growth rate below that of the private sector.[9]

Much of the productivity growth and resultant employment shift reflects technical progress and capital investment. Some of the employment shift also stems from changes in society's consumption demands. The move toward a service economy is by no means confined to the United States; similar trends can be found in other developed countries. These fundamental trends can be expected to continue—regardless of international trade developments. Certainly, the U.S. employment pattern in the year 2000 will look substantially different than the current structure.

The fact that a long-term trend has developed does not make it a good thing, and the fact that international trade has played a relatively small role in creating the trend does not mean that trade policy can be ignored. *If* the trend is undesirable, then steps to reverse it may be worth undertaking. *If* it could be shown that a restrictive trade policy would accomplish such an end, then a case might be made for implementation of protective measures.

Some of the arguments against the drift toward a service economy are loosely based on national security considerations. For example, it is said that the United States cannot afford to be too dependent on foreign suppliers of oil as shown by the politically inspired embargo by Arab oil-exporting nations against the United States. Of course, even in such dramatic cases there are policy alternatives to self-sufficiency, such as stockpiling of vital commodities. And the concept of a vital industry can be stretched to nonsensical proportions, as was done in the case of clothespins industry in the 1950s. [10]

In general, however, the argument for resisting the service economy seems less specific. Having a large industrial base is thought to promote national strength and security, even though parts of that base may not be defense-oriented. On these grounds, a case might be made for some sort of generalized trade protection. However, in the nuclear age the tie between industrial strength and international influence is rather loose. Some would argue that protection should be in the form of explicit subsidies voted by Congress rather than hidden subsidies in the form of higher prices induced by tariffs.

The pressure by organized labor for trade restrictions sometimes has been attributed to an institutional interest. Critics of trade restrictions note that unionization is more concentrated in manufacturing than in services and distribution. Spokesmen for organized labor have angrily denied the implication that they are trying to stimulate "their" sector relative to others. [11] In recent years unionization has grown most rapidly in the government sector, an area not directly touched by international trade.

The labor movement has had a long history of workers combining with employers to seek protection from imports. [12] Evidence of such activity goes back to the early days of American independence. For most of its history, however, the American Federation of Labor as an umbrella organization followed its general policy of "voluntarism," avoiding any official position on protection. Internal differences of opinion surfaced from time to time, particularly during the national debate on the Smoot-Hawley Tariff.

In the postwar years, the AFL passed resolutions favoring protection in particular industries, but remained neutral on the general issue. The CIO had even less to say on the subject. By the time of the merger, both groups tended to favor trade liberalization, provided that "international fair labor standards" were maintained. But the issue was not pushed until the Kennedy administration elicited support for the Trade Expansion Act by attaching a program of worker adjustment assistance. Finally, as noted earlier, the official position shifted toward protective quotas and the Burke-Hartke bill.

The historical record suggests that the official positions of the AFL—CIO and its predecessors have been responsive to internal political pressures. As the impact of trade shifts, so does the consensus position. The rise in significant competition in the manufacturing sector, as other countries began to catch up in technology or to develop their industries, led to restricted employment opportunities and greater resistance to wage increases in certain major unions. Thus, official policy swung around from the period when expanded trade was seen as an opportunity for export and employment expansion in the same sectors.

The Unemployment Impact of Trade

The Macro View

Could trade restrictions be used to reduce demand unemployment? Most economists would admit—grudgingly perhaps—that trade restrictions in principle could raise aggregate demand. The mechanism is simple enough. If demand is insufficient, any stimulus will raise production levels and employment opportunities and thereby reduce unemployment. Import restrictions are a stimulus, in that when an industry receives protection, its output tends to rise, as domestic production substitutes partly for foreign imports. "Multiplier" effects can spread the increased production to other sectors of the economy.

There is another side to the question, however. Attempts to reduce unemployment through trade restrictions are not looked at kindly by other countries. Because the United States is such an important element in world trade, open attempts to "export" unemployment through trade restrictions likely would be met with foreign restrictions on U.S. exports. Other countries would not fail to notice any such attempt, since the small size of U.S. exports and imports relative to GNP implies that massive restrictions would have to be undertaken to create a substantial overall effect. Retaliation against U.S. exports would tend to raise unemployment and would lead to adverse multiplier effects.

In addition to potential retaliation, other considerations suggest that trade restrictions are not useful in regulating the economy. Since the 1930s, developed countries have adopted monetary and fiscal policy as the best way to influence aggregate demand. Prior to that time, of course, these instruments were not widely understood and trade restrictions—though they led to trade wars and "beggar thy neighbor" policies—seemed by some to be a logical reaction to general unemployment.

In the modern world, government policy makers usually have some notion of a short-run appropriate target rate of unemployment and economic activity. They attempt to balance off the inflationary effects of holding unemployment "too" low against the public desire to keep unemployment down. There is much controversy about the appropriate target and about the impact of unemployment on inflation. But as long as government policy makers adhere to a target unemployment rate through manipulation of monetary and fiscal policy, protective measures will have little overall effect. If a particular industry succeeded in obtaining increased protection, any aggregate stimulus that resulted presumably would be offset by monetary and fiscal policy to keep the economy on its aggregate target. Reduction in unemployment in one area, therefore, is likely to lead to higher unemployment in some other sector. That is, *in a modern economy, the impact of trade restrictions may simply be to spread unemployment around rather than to lower its absolute level.*

Unfortunately, in recent years empirical discussion of the impact of trade sometimes has lost sight of this fact. Studies have been made—on both sides of the protection issue—which allegedly determine the employment "contribution" of exports or the job "displacement" wrought by imports. Arguments are then based on whether the contribution is greater or less than the displacement, or over the direction of the trend in the difference between them.[13]

The studies themselves are simple enough. If 10 percent of the employment in an industry goes to exports, the statistician simply attributes 10 percent of the employment in that industry to exports. He may even look at indirect "input-output" effects to determine what other industries feed production to the export industry and allocate some of their employment to exports. A similar tabulation can be made to determine what employment would have been involved in producing substitutes for imports, if the imports had not been available.

Such studies are fine for delving into theoretical aspects of comparative advantage along the lines of the Leontief investigation cited earlier and are useful in analyzing the structural problems of particular industries. But such studies are not useful to measure the *aggregate* effect of trade on employment or unemployment at the national level. Demand unemployment may be attributed to the monetary and fiscal policy which the government has chosen, but not to the activity or hypothetical activity of some particular sector of the economy. An example from an actual study would be useful. Table 1.2 shows the results of a tabulation by the Bureau of Labor Statistics of the employment "attributable" to exports in 1971. According to the table, some 3.5 million jobs were "attributable" to exports in that year. But suppose the export market dried up. The table shows that the manufacturing sector would feel a greater impact than the communications and public utilities sector (1,654,000 jobs versus 69,000). But if the export sector did not exist, it would be wrong to assume that there would be another 3.5 million jobless workers. Some industries would be smaller and others would be larger, but if the

Table 1.2. Jobs "Attributed" Directly and Indirectly to Exports of All Sectors by Sector, 1971 (thousands of jobs)

Sector	Direct effect*	Indirect effect†	Total
Agriculture, forestry, and fisheries	230	155	385
Manufacturing	956	698	1,654
Nonmanufacturing, except agriculture	709	794	1,503
Construction	‡	42	42
Mining	32	50	83
Transportation	259	109	368
Communications and public utilities	12	57	69
Wholesale and retail trade	197	186	389
Other services	199	298	498
Government enterprises	10	52	61
Total	1,895	1,647	3,542

SOURCE: D.P. Eldridge and N. C. Saunders, "Employment and Exports, 1963-72," *Monthly Labor Review* 96 (August 1973):16-27, especially pp. 18, 20–22.

*Jobs in export industries.
†Jobs producing inputs sold to export industries.
‡Less than 500 jobs.
NOTE: Details need not sum to totals due to rounding.

government followed a policy of stabilizing the unemployment rate, joblessness in this hypothetical state of the economy would not necessarily be higher.

The Micro View

Although tabulations such as those of table 1.2 are not useful in dealing with unemployment caused by deficient aggregate demand, they can be helpful in analyzing structural unemployment associated with foreign trade. An increase in imports or a drop in export demand can lead to structural problems, and data on which industries are particularly prone to such difficulties may be useful to policy makers.

Structural unemployment problems arise when normal labor turnover and mobility in an industry are insufficient to handle a drop in its demand for labor. Structural problems associated with trade are no different from structural problems resulting from other causes. An industry characterized by an older work force whose skills are heavily industry-specific obviously is prone to structural unemployment.

By their nature, structural problems are localized, not general. In some cases, the appropriate remedy may well be some form of import restriction. Alternatives such as adjustment assistance or manpower retraining programs may not work in cases of severe worker immobility. Presumably, however, such restrictions can be transitional, designed to phase themselves out as the problem recedes. Moreover, it is important not to assume that severe immobility will be a problem in all instances. Even in the recession year of 1974, when unemployment averaged 5.6 percent, voluntary quit rates in manufacturing averaged 2.3 percent per *month*. A recent Labor Department survey revealed that median time on the current jobs was less than five years for men and less than three years for women.[14] Fifteen percent of the unemployed in 1974 were job leavers, and 42 percent were new entrants or re-entrants to the labor force. Fluidity, not stagnation, characterizes the American labor force.

16

Conclusions

Although economists tend to favor unrestricted trade, there is no guarantee—even in the standard economic models—that labor automatically gains from trade. It is conceivable, although by no means certain, that recent changes in U.S. trade patterns may have had an adverse effect on labor. Further discussion of this possibility is reserved for Chapter 2. Clearly, at the micro level, instances of structural unemployment due to shift in foreign trade patterns can and sometimes have occurred.

The appropriate remedy for labor-related trade problems however, is not necessarily trade restriction. Moreover, the political process is not especially adept at handling such difficulties. Trade policy tends to respond to short-run pressures brought about by interest group coalitions. In recent years, the net balance of these pressures generally has favored trade expansion, although organized labor has not been part of the coalition.

When strong economic interests are involved, the possibility of dispassionate debate diminishes. The positions vary from strongly felt assertions that freer trade is always desirable to apocalyptic visions of a powerless nation of hamburger stands. The public debate is not aided by the veneer of complicated theory surrounding international economics. For the manpower specialist, the best advice is to treat trade-related problems just as domestic problems would be treated. Every proposed remedy to a problem has costs and benefits to be evaluated even if these cannot always be quantified. Some questions, such as the distribution of national income or the appropriate inflation-unemployment trade-off, go beyond the traditional scope of manpower programs. These questions are ultimately political and must be settled in that arena. But structural unemployment problems, whether caused by foreign trade, new technology, or shifts in public taste, should be amenable to sectoral remedies.

2

The Labor Content of U.S. Trade

Introduction

The factor-supply explanation of the pattern of U.S. trade might provide a long-run rationale for the recent pressure by organized labor for import restrictions. According to that approach, the United States *ought* to be importing labor-intensive goods and exporting capital-intensive goods. If that occurred and as trade grew in significance, the result might be downward pressure on real wages. Wages might not fall in absolute terms; they might rise somewhat more slowly than in the past.

Chapter 1 pointed out that the factor-supply explanation has *not* been supported by previous empirical work. Imports in fact appeared to be capital-intensive relative to exports in the Leontief and subsequent investigations, suggesting that labor as a class should be benefiting from trade. The problem with the earlier investigations is that trade patterns were abnormal during the years studied. There was great disruption in the aftermath of World War II and during the period of European recovery. Technological sophistication in Europe and Japan was below the U.S. level, and many trade barriers were erected after the war. By the late 1960s, however, the Kennedy Round tariff reductions and the spread of technology by multinational firms and other mechanisms may have eased the distortions.

Normality is difficult to define. A case could be made that the international market was disrupted again in the early 1970s. The dollar was devalued twice, creating currency speculation and uncertainty about the future course of the international monetary system. Wage and price controls created artificial incentives to export and import in some industries. Finally, the oil embargo disrupted trade and production in 1973 and 1974. As a result, the best years to look for underlying trends are those of the late 1960s. For this reason, the evidence cited below is based on a comparison of 1965 and 1970, years surrounding the Kennedy Round. That evidence suggests that the Leontief paradox had evaporated, or at least was evaporating, by 1970.

Evidence from Trade in Manufactures

What kinds of pressures do exports put on the labor force? What kinds of skills and wage levels are involved in their production? Similarly, what kinds of pressures would be put on the labor force if imported items were produced domestically? These questions can be approached by estimating the export and import labor forces, based on the industries that actually are the exporters, or that hypothetically would be called on to produce substitutes for imports. Export and import labor forces can be estimated for any sector, or for the economy as a whole. This section centers on manufacturing, since more detailed data are available for that sector than for the overall economy.

Tables 2.1 and 2.2 compare the export and import labor forces for manufacturing trade based on the pattern of trade existing in 1965 and 1970. In each calculation a base year has been selected for which labor requirements are calculated. These overall requirements have then been broken into demographic and other characteristics based on the utilization patterns of the industries involved.[1] The absolute composition of the labor forces and their absolute and relative changes between the two years can be compared.

Whether the 1965 or the 1970 trade pattern is used, some basic characteristics of the export and import forces are apparent from table 2.1. The export labor force tends to be more

19

Table 2.1. Selected Labor Force and Industrial Characteristics, U.S. Manufacturing Exports and Imports*

Characteristic	U.S. trade with	1965 Exp.	1965 Imp.	1970 Exp.	1970 Imp.
Production workers	World	78.8	81.7	76.8	81.4
as % of employment	Japan	79.8	83.2	79.4	83.2
Average hourly earnings,	World	2.81	2.51	2.82	2.47
production workers ($)	Japan	2.78	2.37	2.66	2.46
Annual compensation per	World	7759	6957	7832	7181
full-time equivalent employee ($)	Japan	7532	6743	7314	7126
Union workers as %	World	44.0	48.3	45.1	49.1
of employment	Japan	45.2	47.7	45.0	48.0
Female workers as %	World	22.4	27.9	22.7	29.6
of employment	Japan	19.5	35.1	19.7	34.1
Full-time workers as %	World	74.8	71.5	74.8	70.9
of employment	Japan	71.0	69.7	68.3	70.4
Nonwhite workers as %	World	8.4	10.3	8.6	10.2
of employment	Japan	10.5	10.4	11.7	9.7
Median years of age	World	40.0	40.7	39.8	40.2
(weighted average)	Japan	40.0	40.1	39.5	39.4
Median years of education	World	12.1	11.8	12.2	11.9
(weighted average)	Japan	12.0	11.8	11.9	12.0
College-educated workers	World	8.7	6.3	9.5	6.6
as % of employment	Japan	9.1	6.0	8.7	7.3
Northeast workers as %	World	29.1	32.8	29.9	32.7
of employment	Japan	28.0	36.5	29.0	34.6
North Central workers as	World	36.9	28.1	35.1	32.5
% of employment	Japan	30.2	28.8	26.9	34.3
Southern workers as %	World	21.3	26.6	21.0	24.0
of employment	Japan	22.4	25.7	23.1	22.7
Western workers as % of	World	12.6	12.4	14.0	10.8
employment	Japan	19.4	9.0	21.0	8.5
Ratio of establishments	World	10.7	11.2	10.3	11.3
with 100 or more workers to	Japan	4.2	13.1	3.3	13.6
total establishments (%)					
Industrial Concentration Index,	World	2.3	2.3	2.4	2.3
1 = low; 4 = high	Japan	2.3	2.3	2.2	2.4

SOURCE: See note 1.

*Excludes ordnance.

Table 2.2.   Selected Characteristics Relating to Labor-Intensity,
U.S. Manufacturing Exports and Imports*

Characteristic	U.S. trade with	1965		1970	
		Exp.	Imp.	Exp.	Imp.
Payroll as %	World	23.1	20.1	23.7	20.8
of sales	Japan	22.0	24.9	24.7	23.8
Employee compensation	World	28.9	26.7	29.2	27.8
as % of sales	Japan	26.8	30.6	29.5	31.3
Payroll as % of	World	46.4	46.6	46.5	47.7
value added	Japan	44.9	51.7	47.0	49.1
Employee compensation as %	World	68.3	67.8	68.5	68.9
of national income origi-	Japan	66.0	72.8	67.5	72.8
nating plus depreciation					
Book value of capital	World	10,669	13,390	10,667	10,884
per employee ($)	Japan	12,075	8,877	10,089	8,159
Book value of capital	World	13,547	16,389	13,890	13,378
per production worker ($)	Japan	15,130	10,669	12,714	9,795
Book value of capital per pro-	World	7.11	8.28	7.18	6.75
duction worker man-hour ($)	Japan	8.24	5.42	6.77	5.04
Depreciation per full-time	World	974	1,060	955	944
equivalent employee ($)	Japan	1,131	723	968	711
Horsepower per	World	13.7	19.0	13.9	14.1
production worker	Japan	16.1	11.7	14.1	10.0

SOURCE: See note 1.
*Excludes ordnance.

highly educated and more highly paid than the import labor force. It tends to be younger, "whiter," and features a lower ratio of production workers to total employed than the import labor force. These findings are in keeping with previous studies that suggest that U.S. exports are more intensive in human capital than are imports.

The manufacturing import labor force tends to be somewhat more unionized, more feminine, and to consist of more nonwhite workers than the export labor force. It contains a lower proportion of full-time workers who seem to be slightly older than those in the export labor force. These various characteristics are not independent of one another, of course.

Regional characteristics of the export and import labor forces are also in general accord with the other labor force characteristics. In view of the relatively higher pay of the export labor force, it is less southern and northeastern than the import labor force.

Since unionization is roughly associated with size of establishment, the manufacturing export labor force is less likely to be found in medium-to-large establishments (one hundred or more workers) than the import labor force. A crude index of industrial concentration (dominance of a few firms in the product market) was calculated on a three-digit basis with the value "four" representing high concentration.[2] The index shows little difference between exports and imports, but this is not surprising given its method of calculation.

Table 2.1 permits a comparison between the manufacturing trade patterns of 1965 and 1970. During the late 1960s, both exports and imports tended to move toward sectors that were more heavily unionized and had more highly educated workers. There was some movement in imports toward sectors with lower-paid production workers. However, annual 1965 compensation per full-time equivalent employee at *all* occupational levels rose slightly when tabulated with the 1970 import pattern. This presumably reflects the trend toward industries with more college-educated workers. The import labor force became somewhat more feminine, reflecting increased textile and apparel imports, but despite this increase, the import labor force shifted toward the North Central heavy-manufacturing heartland. Growth in imports of transportation equipment played an important role in this shift.

Table 2.2 summarizes a variety of measures relating to the degree of labor-intensity of manufacturing exports and imports. Industries with relatively low capital-to-labor ratios might be expected to exhibit relatively high ratios of payroll to sales or payroll to value added. The absolute values of such ratios are only imperfect proxies for labor-intensity, however, since they also reflect differences in the average industry wage and return on capital. Such ratios are more interesting in terms of the *changes* that occur as the result of the differences in the composition of the 1965 and 1970 trade patterns. The various ratios reported in the first four rows of table 2.3 seem to imply some increase in the labor-intensity of imports due to changing import composition. The ratios also move upward for exports, although the shift is smaller than for imports.

It is probably best to confront the capital-to-labor ratio directly. Apart from the well-known theoretical complexities, "capital" is an elusive concept in empirical studies. One available measure is the gross book value of depreciable assets. This index, of course, represents a stock rather than a flow. The closest approximations to the "using up" of capital for production are the capital consumption allowances (depreciation) reported in the national income accounts. This measure,

Table 2.3. Large Manufacturing Import Product Classes Showing Real Increases of 100 Percent or More, 1965–1970*

Product	Horsepower per production worker, 1962 requirements
Meat products	5.9
Weaving mill products, synthetic	6.9
Yarn and thread mill products	9.1
Men's and boy's furnishings	.2
Women's and misses' outerwear	.1
Furniture and fixtures, NEC†	4.2
Basic chemicals	93.6
Rubber footwear	3.4
Plastic products	8.5
Footwear except rubber	1.0
Radio and T.V. receiving equipment	2.8
Communications equipment	5.4
Electronics components	2.3
Electronics products, NEC	4.8
Motor vehicles	11.1
Transportation equipment, NEC	2.6
Photographic equipment	8.9
Toys and sporting goods	3.5
Miscellaneous manufactures	1.9

*Product classes considered "large" if they accounted for $100 million or more of imports in 1970.
†NEC means not elsewhere classified.

unfortunately, is affected by accounting conventions and tax laws. The horsepower rating of power equipment used in production is a third possible measure. It represents a stock measure since horsepower "ratings" are reported—based on 1962 requirements—rather than power consumption.

All of these measures, when tabulated into capital-to-labor ratios, suggest an increase in the labor-intensity of manufacturing imports during the 1965–70 period. They produce ambiguous results concerning exports alone, but all suggest that exports were labor-intensive *relative* to imports in 1965, but that the pattern reversed or tended to reverse by 1970.

Table 2.3 provides a listing of the major import product classes in the manufacturing sector that rose rapidly in volume during 1965–70 and that represented a significant portion of total imports. The textile, apparel, electronics, footwear, and other industries listed on table 2.3 are all relatively labor-intensive. The major exceptions are basic chemicals, which is not very labor-intensive, and motor vehicles, which is about average in labor-intensity compared with the rest of manufacturing.

In contrast, table 2.4 shows that the major export product classes that grew rapidly during 1965–70 show a broad scatter of labor-intensities. Some are below and some are above the manufacturing mean of 12.3 horsepower per production worker. The motor vehicle industry manages to appear as a major growth export and import during the same period. This growth was due to the 1965 agreement with Canada that integrated the North American auto industry by permitting free trade in new cars and parts.

Overall Trade

Not all the earlier calculations could be repeated when trade in mining and agricultural products was added to manufacturing trade. However, table 2.5 indicates that important conclusions about manufacturing hold generally when the other sectors are included. The export labor force is relatively higher paid and better educated than the import labor force. It is somewhat less

Table 2.4.   Large Manufacturing Export Product Classes Showing Real
Increases of 65 Percent or More, 1965–1970*

Product	Horsepower per production worker, 1962 requirements
Lumber and wood products	16.7
Pulp mill products	101.9
Paper and paperboard products	7.8
Drugs	11.7
Agricultural chemicals	29.1
Rubber products, NEC	11.5
Metal stampings	8.4
Office machines including computers	3.4
Radio and T.V. receiving equipment	2.8
Communications equipment	5.4
Electronics components	2.3
Motor vehicles	11.1
Aircraft and parts	7.4
Photographic equipment	8.9
Jewelry and silverware including diamonds	3.5

*Product classes considered "large" if they accounted for $100 million or more of exports in 1970.

highly unionized than the import labor force and has a smaller proportion of nonwhites and part-time workers. In 1965 exports were relatively less labor-intensive than imports as measured by the ratio of depreciation per full-time equivalent employee.

During the period 1965–70, the labor-intensity of the import labor force rose relative to that of the export labor force. Based on 1965 industry characteristics, the Leontief paradox appears to have vanished by 1970.[3] Unionization of both export and import industries rose, but the effect was sharper in imports as import of manufactured goods outpaced the growth of agricultural imports. The relatively low rates of female employment in agriculture and mining made the import labor force somewhat less feminine than the export labor force in 1965 (based on 1970 industry characteristics). By 1970, however, the rapid growth in imported manufactures, especially in textiles and apparel, reversed the relative femininity of the export labor force.

25

Table 2.5.   Selected Characteristics, U.S. Exports and Imports in
Agriculture, Mining, and Manufacturing*

Characteristic	U.S. trade with	1965 Exp.	1965 Imp.	1970 Exp.	1970 Imp.
Employee compensation	World	25.3	22.8	26.3	25.3
as % of sales	Japan	20.0	29.8	24.2	31.0
Employee compensation as %	World	55.8	55.2	58.4	61.2
of national income origi-	Japan	41.8	70.1	49.2	71.6
nating plus depreciation					
Annual compensation per	World	6,734	6,199	7,004	6,715
full-time equivalent	Japan	5,408	6,605	5,941	7,063
employee ($)					
Depreciation per full-	World	1,329	1,421	1,249	1,178
time equivalent employee ($)	Japan	1,827	783	1,553	737
Union workers as %	World	29.3	34.1	32.6	40.0
of employment	Japan	18.6	44.6	24.2	46.7
Female workers as %	World	21.4	20.3	21.6	24.1
of employment	Japan	17.2	34.9	18.0	34.0
Full-time workers as %	World	74.6	73.4	74.7	72.3
of employment	Japan	72.1	69.6	70.6	70.5
Nonwhite workers as %	World	8.9	11.2	9.0	10.8
of employment	Japan	11.1	10.4	11.6	9.7
Median years of age	World	40.3	40.8	40.0	40.3
(weighted average)	Japan	40.5	40.1	40.2	39.4
Median years of education	World	11.9	11.6	12.0	11.8
(weighted average)	Japan	11.5	11.7	11.5	11.9
College-educated workers	World	8.2	5.8	8.9	6.2
as % of employment	Japan	7.5	6.0	7.3	7.3

SOURCE: See note 1.
*Excludes ordnance.

Trade with Japan

American trade with Japan in both directions expanded
rapidly from 1965 to 1970. The proportion of American exports
going to Japan relative to total exports rose from 7.5 percent to
10.8 percent during this period. Imports from Japan represented
11.3 percent of the U.S. import total in 1965 and rose to 14.7
percent by 1970. This two-way expansion was not without its

pains. There were complaints that exports of lumber to Japan put a price squeeze on U.S. homebuilding. Coal exports created demands for export quotas. At the same time, Japanese competition in manufactured goods brought pressure for import restrictions. Fears of "unemployment—made in Japan" were expressed.

Within manufacturing, the export and import labor forces involving trade with Japan have a number of the characteristics of the all-country-trade labor forces (table 2.1). The export-to-Japan labor force was more highly paid, had more college education, was less feminine, and less unionized than its import counterpart. On the other hand, the tendency of exports to Japan to involve smaller establishments (based on number of employees) relative to imports was more pronounced than for overall U.S. trade. This tendency reflects the substantial concentration of U.S. exports to Japan in the lumber sector, where small establishments are common. The lumber sector is also responsible for the relative concentration of export-to-Japan employment in the western states.

Table 2.2 indicates that manufacturing imports from Japan were relatively labor-intensive compared with exports, even at the start of the period considered. Both the import and export trade pattern with Japan tended to shift toward labor-intensive industries during 1965–70. The impact of both the shift in the pattern of Japanese manufacturing trade and the increased volume of that trade was sufficient to account for the reversal of the labor-intensity of all-country imports relative to all-country exports in manufacturing.

When all exports to, and imports from, Japan are compared with the overall all-country trade pattern (table 2.5), a number of interesting contrasts emerge. The import-from-Japan labor force was strikingly more unionized and more feminine than either the overall all-country import labor force or the export-to-Japan labor force. The export-to-Japan labor force was *lower* paid than the import-from-Japan labor force and was older. In 1970, the index of median years of education indicates somewhat more human capital embodied in the import-from-Japan labor force than in export-to-Japan employment. As in the case of manufacturing alone, imports from Japan were more labor-intensive than exports to Japan. When Japanese trade is excluded from overall all-country trade (table 2.4), relative labor-intensity appears not to have reversed by 1970. Depreciation per full-time equivalent employed remained higher in imports than in exports in 1970, based on the 1965 factor-use pattern. Thus the growth of the volume and shift in the pattern of trade with Japan played an important role in overturning the Leontief paradox.[4]

Significance of the Findings

The tables in this chapter do not present the labor content of trade in absolute form. That is, the data are reported in terms of proportions (for example, percent of college graduates in the export or import labor force) or ratios. This style of presentation was chosen for two reasons. The first is technical: input/output analysis was not applied and therefore indirect labor and capital inputs were not included. The impact of not using input/output analysis is relatively small when proportions and ratios are computed, but can be large for absolute estimates. Second, and more important, absolute calculations are suggestive of the "job-counting" literature heavily criticized in Chapter 1. Changes in the absolute magnitudes of the export and import labor forces provide little indication of whether total employment was increased or decreased. The total employment effect is a function of worker mobility and turnover and of aggregate demand policy on the part of the government. Structural characteristics are best captured by the proportions and ratios presented in the tables in this chapter.

Table 2.5 reinforces the general findings of the earlier studies of labor characteristics discussed in Chapter 1. Workers in import-competing industries—as reflected in the hypothetical import labor force—are somewhat less educated and are paid less than workers in export industries or in the economy as a whole. These findings suggest less "human capital" in the import-competing industries than elsewhere. Median age was slightly higher than the national average for workers in the import-competing sector.

Such characteristics provide "mixed" signals for the manpower specialist. If a "typical" import-competing worker is involuntarily displaced, the burden inflicted on him may be especially heavy. On the other hand, low-wage workers and low-wage industries often display higher quit rates than higher-paid workers and high-wage industries. Hence, paradoxically, a given percentage decline in employment may create less involuntary displacement in some import-competing industries than in other industries. Similarly, import-competing workers are more likely to be full-time employees than are workers in the overall economy. This characteristic suggests a greater importance of earnings of import-competing workers to their total family incomes. On the other hand, the higher rate of unionization in the import-competing sector suggests that the older workers with dependents in that sector are more likely to be protected by seniority systems. Displacement is therefore more likely to occur among younger workers for whom mobility may be easier.

The "mixed" characteristics of import-competing workers suggest that the study of trade-related unemployment is best conducted at the micro level. Characteristics of a particular *group* of displaced workers are the best guide to appropriate public policy. Depending on these characteristics, the manpower specialists might recommend options ranging from adjustment assistance to import protection.

Questions of displacement through trade are inherently short run. The findings of this chapter, however, are suggestive of some longer-run trends. There did appear to be evidence that imports were becoming labor-intensive relative to exports in the late 1960s. As noted in Chapter 1, such a trend conceivably could have a long-run adverse effect on labor's welfare in terms of real income. Of course, the analysis upon which such a conclusion might be drawn is based on a highly abstract economic model, and it would be unwise to accept its predictions without question. No one can be certain of the long-run impact of trade on the overall income distribution. But the fact that organized labor's concern with trade developed during the period when the U.S. trade structure seemed to change suggests that labor leaders felt some pressures in labor-intensive sectors. Whether the trends of the 1960s will continue remains to be seen. The transitory factors that influenced U.S. trade in the early 1970s would tend to camouflage underlying pressures.

Trade Patterns and Illegal Immigration

Manpower specialists recently have become concerned with a phenomenon that has an indirect relationship to trade trends. Trade theory suggests that flows of labor and capital are substitutes for trade. Put simply, you can either import people and capital and consume their domestic output, or you can combine the capital and labor abroad and import their output. In crude terms, the United States followed the first model during the nineteenth and early twentieth centuries and in some ways has moved to the second model more recently.

Of course, immigration and trade are not interchangeable. Immigrants present social problems, particularly when breadwinners bring their families, which goods do not. But both immigration and trade may respond to the same underlying force: international wage differentials. For example, the American-Mexican wage differential has led to both trade (through items 806.30 and 807.00 of the Tariff Schedules described in Chapter 5) and immigration, the latter largely illegal.

Until fairly recently, much of the illegal alien work force was confined to agriculture in states bordering Mexico, a leftover from the bracero program.[5] Recent evidence, however, indicates that the problem has spread from agriculture to other industries and from rural areas to urban centers. The illegals come not only from Mexico, but from other Latin American countries, the Caribbean, and Asia.

If analysis is confined to wage impacts, trade policies and immigration flows may well be interconnected. In some industries, the presence of low-wage sources of imports limits the competitive wage level that these labor-intensive industries can pay in the United States. Illegal aliens—who come from low-wage countries—provide a labor supply that may still find such depressed wage levels attractive. If illegal immigration were cut off, the reaction might be greater imports of labor-intensive goods and a lower production level of such goods in the United States.[6]

Conclusions on the connections between trade and illegal immigration necessarily are speculative. The only data available indicate the industries in which raids by immigration authorities take place. These data indicate that the problem extends beyond farming.

3

Worker Adjustment Assistance Legislation

Development of Trade Adjustment Assistance

Since the early 1960s, the federal government nominally has pursued a policy of providing "adjustment assistance" to firms and workers injured by imports. It is not surprising that the original program did not live up to its promise; many manpower programs created in the 1960s also proved to be disappointments. But the genesis and operation of the adjustment assistance effort is worth reviewing, since the program remains part of federal policy under the recently enacted Trade Act of 1974.

Adjustment assistance—although its official rationale is compensation of those hurt by trade—covers only a specific type of injury. Workers who benefit from the program are those who are actually "displaced," that is, who become unemployed because of trade. If trade had a more gradual, long-run effect of retarding the growth in real wages, adjustment assistance would not alleviate the problem. It is to help only individuals who are overtly injured, not to assist a broad class. In the early 1950s, when the adjustment assistance concept was first developed, exports were definitely labor-intensive relative to imports. Major elements of the unionized, heavy-industry sector looked on themselves as export-oriented. Most unions, if they considered the issue, probably viewed expanded trade as creating employment for their sectors.

Adjustment assistance was first proposed by David J. McDonald, then president of the United Steelworkers, in a 1954 minority report issued by a special government commission.[1] At the time, U.S. trade policy was caught in a battle between the administration and Congress. The administration generally favored trade negotiations and tariff reductions. But Congress, reacting to pressures from domestic import-competing industries, had included in the tariff law various "escape-clause" provisions that potentially could nullify negotiated tariff concessions. Injured industries could complain to the Tariff Commission. If, after an investigation, an injury was found to have occurred, semiautomatic tariff increases would follow. McDonald's suggestion was simply that instead of the escape-clause approach, injured workers, firms, and communities should be given federal financial aid. Workers would receive unemployment benefits, retraining and relocation allowances, and job counseling. Firms would receive technical and financial benefits—including favorable tax treatment. Communities would receive preference for government contracts.

The McDonald recommendation appeared quite radical at the time it was made, but it found some support in Congress, notably among Senators John F. Kennedy, Hubert Humphrey, and Paul Douglas. The program did not become law, however, until it was included in the 1962 Trade Expansion Act. By that time, the notion of an active manpower policy had gained favor—the Manpower Development and Training Act also was passed in 1962—and the McDonald proposal seemed less startling.

During the congressional hearings on the Trade Expansion Act (TEA), the AFL-CIO officially endorsed passage. President Meany—in supporting documents—noted that the AFL-CIO's 1961 convention had officially supported the TEA. The convention resolution pointedly noted: "Adequate assistance or relief for those adversely affected by imports is essential if the

American labor movement is to continue its support for a liberal trade program."[2] Individual unions also supported the proposed bill. McDonald of the Steelworkers recalled his original recommendation in expressing his union's endorsement of the bill. Favorable testimony also was heard from the Electrical Workers and the Automobile Workers. Not all unions supported the TEA. Unions in such import-competing fields as glassware, hats, leather, and pottery opposed the bill. The largest labor union to oppose the TEA was the Teamsters, whose opposition probably stemmed from the conflict between their president James Hoffa and the Kennedy administration. Much of the Teamsters' opposition revolved around the charge that the TEA gave too much power to the president.[3]

The major business groups supported trade liberalization, but not the adjustment assistance features incorporated in the TEA. Four points of opposition were expressed by the National Association of Manufacturers:

1) Adjustment assistance seems to imply that there is something wrong with the operation of the free market. . . .
2) Business enterprises and their employees are continuously affected, for better or worse, by all sorts of events beyond their control. . . . We . . . oppose singling out any one of these possibilities as a basis of a special program of Federal assistance.
3) It is impossible to trace out all the effects of any given tariff change . . . . Judgments as to which firms or persons would be entitled to special assistance would inevitably be arbitrary . . . .
4) All experience warns that programs of this type inevitably expand and proliferate.[4]

As might be expected in a debate on a far-reaching bill, it is sometimes hard to sort out the "real" issues from the smoke screens. A reading of the hearings in the House and Senate suggests that some opponents of trade reform seized on the adjustment assistance provisions as a handy point of controversy. A number of state directors of unemployment compensation were brought forward to charge that adjustment assistance to workers represented an attempt to "federalize" unemployment insurance. To counteract this charge, other state officials were trotted out to support the bill. An issue was raised concerning whether adjustment assistance was legally a form of unemployment compensation; some claimed that such an interpretation would prevent many states from administering the benefits for the secretary of labor. (In actual practice, the Department of Labor managed to negotiate its way around the issue in its dealings with state agencies.) Much of the opposition to the TEA faded when the president announced a new program of "voluntary" textile export limits by Japan.

For reasons to be described below, adjustment assistance did not remain a political success. No workers were found eligible for assistance until 1969, and payments did not begin to flow until mid-1970. Hence, any hope of retaining labor support for continued trade liberalization on the basis of adjustment assistance collapsed. In retrospect, it appears that much of the difficulty in implementing the program stemmed from its essentially political purpose. Perhaps if adjustment assistance had been viewed as an important program in its own right—and not simply a way of selling trade reform—the TEA would have been written more carefully.

An example in the mid-1960s of what a better-drafted bill could do was a special agreement between the United States and Canada signed in early 1965 providing for free trade in new automobiles and parts. To implement the agreement, Congress passed the Automotive Products Trade Act of 1965 (APTA), which contained special provisions for adjustment assistance. The APTA's adjustment assistance provisions were successful both politically and in terms of delivery to the intended recipients. Politically, the United Automobile Workers—which had members in both the U.S. and Canadian automobile industries—was able to support the APTA. (Similar arrangements for adjustment assistance were established in Canada.) The APTA provided sufficient assistance that it has been cited as an example of a successful program. When its assistance terms expired at the end of fiscal 1968, it had become a "model" bill.[5]

Major trade legislation was not passed again until late 1974. Again, as with the TEA, the European Common Market provided an incentive for new negotiations. With the admission of Britain and the other states that followed, the European Economic Community included nine countries with a population of 260 million. The EEC concluded special tariff agreements on manufactured goods with other European countries. At the same time, with the lowering of tariffs under the Kennedy Round, more and more concern was voiced about nontariff barriers, which previously had not been explicitly considered in U.S. trade legislation. The Trade Act of 1974 (TA) provided new negotiating authority for the president, both on tariff and nontariff barriers. It provided for generalized tariff preferences, such as duty-free treatment of the products of less-developed countries over a ten-year period and most-favored nation treatment for imports from those communist countries not currently enjoying that status.

When the TA was considered initially, administration unhappiness with the adjustment assistance concept took the form of proposed lowered benefits rather than their immediate elimination.[6] But these benefits were to be eliminated as state unemployment benefits were raised to administration-endorsed levels. Ultimately, the benefits were raised above TEA provisions, first in the House and again in the Senate. Adjustment assistance did not become a major issue, however, during the course of the debate on the TA, probably because the program already was in existence. In addition, the sponsors of trade liberalization—including major business interests—realized that enhanced benefits would help to obtain passage of the bill.

The change in business attitudes was undoubtedly a crucial factor in the eventual outcome of the TA. Several official government reports had recommended a liberalization of the original TEA program. The president's special trade representative—who headed the American Kennedy Round team of negotiators—submitted a report in 1969 recommending improved access to adjustment assistance.[7] Comments included in the report by business representatives of the Public Advisory Committee on Trade Policy indicate that a revised consensus in the business community was already taking shape. Similarly, the 1971 report of the Commission on International Trade and

Investment Policy (Williams Commission) recommended both improved access to benefits and more generous benefits.[8]

During the hearings on the TA, the revised business attitude became official. The National Association of Manufacturers (NAM) submitted its own proposals for adjustment assistance.[9] While not endorsing a specific liberalization of benefits, the NAM did approve less restrictive eligibility requirements and a speedup of delivery. Quite candidly, the report submitted by the NAM notes that its drafters initially opposed the concept of adjustment assistance. When faced with the alternatives—the threat of the Burke-Hartke bill is mentioned repeatedly in the report—they decided to take a positive approach. The NAM report opposed adjustment assistance to communities and supported assistance to firms (which the administration's original bill omitted).

U.S. Chamber of Commerce representatives supported increased delivery speed and easier eligibility requirements for worker adjustment assistance. The Chamber supported the administration's original bill, which would have generally reduced benefits below the TEA levels and folded them into a standardized unemployment insurance system. Unlike the NAM, the Chamber supported community assistance.[10] Neither the NAM nor the Chamber supported what might be regarded as a liberal program, although many Chamber members favored a more liberal approach.[11] But the position of both groups represented a change in attitudes which—combined with tacit labor support—ensures the continuance of the adjustment assistance program for many years to come.

Adjustment Assistance Provision under Three Trade Acts

Administration

Each of the three major trade acts, the Trade Expansion Act of 1962, the Automotive Products Trade Act of 1965, and the Trade Act of 1974, has provided for a different method of administering adjustment assistance.[12] These are summarized in table 3.1. The APTA prescribed the same benefits for workers and firms as did the TEA, but liberalized the terms of

Table 3.1. Administrative Adjustment Assistance Provisions of Three Trade Acts

	Trade Expansion Act of 1962	Automotive Products Trade Act of 1965	Trade Act of 1974
Coverage	All workers and firms	Workers and firms in the automotive products industry	All workers, firms, and communities
Investigatory body	Tariff Commission	Tariff Commission	Workers: Labor Department Firms: Commerce Department Communities: Commerce Department
Determination of statutory injury	Tariff Commission	President	Workers: Labor Department Firms: Commerce Department Communities: Commerce Department
Certification	President	President	Workers: Labor Department Firms: Commerce Department Communities: Commerce Department
Eligibility determination for individual workers	Labor Department	Labor Department	Labor Department
Administration of payments and benefits	Workers: State unemployment compensation authorities and employment services Firms: Commerce Department and other appropriate agencies	Workers: State unemployment compensation authorities and employment services Firms: Commerce Department and other appropriate agencies	Workers: State unemployment compensation authorities and employment services Firms: Commerce Department, Small Business Administration Communities: Commerce Department and Trade Impacted Area Council
Source of funds	General revenue	General revenue	Workers: Customs duties through Adjustment Assistance Trust Fund Firms: General revenue Communities: General revenue through Community Adjustment Assistance Fund
Termination of program	Early 1975	June 30, 1968	Workers: September 30, 1982 Firms: September 30, 1982 Communities: September 30, 1980

eligibility for applicants in the automotive industry. (Automotive applicants remained eligible to apply under TEA provisions when the assistance sections of the APTA expired in June 1968.) The TA, in contrast, liberalized both eligibility requirements and benefits allowed for all industries and provided adjustment assistance for trade-impacted communities for the first time.

Under terms of the TEA, workers and firms first applied to the Tariff Commission, which then conducted an investigation—limited to a maximum duration of sixty days—to determine eligibility under TEA criteria. If a majority of the commission found the circumstances met TEA criteria, the president was permitted to certify the applicant for aid. Under a pre-existing administrative practice, the president also certified applicants in cases where the Tariff Commission split by a tie vote.

Certification of a group of workers as injured by imports within the meaning of the TEA completed the first stage of the investigation. Within a group of injured workers, however, some subgroups might not be eligible. Hence, there still remained the task of determining individual worker eligibility, and if eligibility existed, the amounts and nature of benefits. The administering of these remaining steps was left to the Department of Labor (technically to the secretary of labor), which contracted with local unemployment insurance and employment service authorities to handle actual benefit administration. Similarly, certified firms had to petition the Department of Commerce for assistance, and the department could deal with other agencies as appropriate. Benefits provided after certification and determination of eligibility were funded from general government revenues.

Under the APTA, the role of the Tariff Commission was reduced to fact-finding, and the allowable duration of a commission investigation was reduced to fifty days. (Additional time was permitted if the president requested further information after the initial report.) Determination of injury and certification were left to the president. Actual decisions were delegated by the president to an Automotive Agreement

Adjustment Assistance Board consisting of the secretaries of labor, commerce, and treasury. In turn, the board delegated its authority to an Automotive Assistance Committee of assistant secretaries from the three departments involved.

The Trade Act of 1974 extended the adjustment program until 1982. It completely removed the Tariff Commission from the handling of adjustment assistance petitions. Presidential action, too, is no longer required. The TA adds assistance to communities through September 1980—a provision not originally endorsed by the Nixon administration. The secretary of commerce handles the entire investigation and certification of these petitions, as well as petitions from firms. (Firm assistance had not been included in the original administration version of the TA, but was restored in the House.) Worker assistance petitions are now to be handled entirely by the secretary of labor. A sixty-day limit applies to all such investigations.

Administration of worker adjustment assistance will continue to be contracted to local authorities. The secretary of commerce may delegate administration of benefits involving smaller companies to the Small Business Administration. Community assistance requires the establishment of a Trade Impacted Area Council at the local level. Members of the council are to include local government, business, labor, and "general public" representatives. Council functions include the establishment of a plan for adjustment assistance and coordination of community action.

Two new trust funds have been created to finance worker and community benefits. Firm benefits continue to come directly from general revenue. For worker benefits, an Adjustment Assistance Trust Fund has been created, with appropriations to come from customs duties. The purpose of using customs revenues is unclear since such revenues far exceed anticipated expenses for worker assistance. Customs revenues, therefore, are not an effective cap on expenditures, and using them rather than a straight allocation of general revenues has no limiting effect on the costs of the program.[13]

General Eligibility

The three trade acts set forth general criteria for eligibility, each in different language. Since this study is concerned primarily with labor problems, only those criteria relating to worker assistance will be discussed. These criteria are summarized in table 3.2. More or less parallel language in the statutes applies to firms (and to communities in the TA).

Under the TEA, a unit of workers applying for adjustment assistance filed a petition with the Tariff Commission. The commission then reviewed the facts surrounding the unit's alleged difficulties against four criteria specified in section 301 (c) of the act. These were: (1) imports "like or directly competitive with" the article the workers produced were increasing in quantity; (2) unemployment or underemployment were occurring or were threatened; (3) the increased imports were the "major factor" in causing or threatening to cause the unemployment or underemployment; (4) the increased imports resulted "in major part" from trade "concessions."

At the time these criteria were placed into TEA, organized labor may have been unaware of the pitfalls they posed. The various phrases in the law already had significance in tariff administration; they meant more than appearances suggested. Only criterion (2) is relatively unambiguous. Most units that applied were already suffering from some unemployment or underemployment at the time they filed for relief.

Criterion (1), for example, requires that imports be shown to have increased. This is simple enough to determine if the workers' product and the imported product are similar. But the workers may produce something that is competitive with a component of an imported product. As the import increases, demand for the product from domestic manufacturers may fall off, and foreign manufacturers may not use American components in their production.

The United Shoe Workers found that the Tariff Commission would not approve a petition on behalf of workers who produced a component of shoes.[14] Imports of foreign-made shoes were increasing, but imports of the component by itself

Table 3.2. Criteria for Worker Unit Eligibility under Three Trade Acts

---
General criteria

Trade Expansion Act of 1962

Eligibility depends on "whether, as a result *in major part* of *concessions* granted under trade agreements, an article *like or directly competitive with* an article produced by such workers' firm, or an appropriate subdivision thereof, is being imported into the United States in such *increased* quantities as to cause, or threaten to cause, unemployment or underemployment of a significant number or proportion of the workers of such firm or subdivision. . . . Increased imports shall be considered to cause, or threated to cause . . . unemployment or underemployment . . . when . . . such increased imports have been the *major factor* in causing, or threatening to cause, such . . . unemployment or underemployment."

Automotive Products Trade Act of 1965

Eligibility depends on a finding that "(1) dislocation of the . . . group of workers has occurred or threatens to occur; (2) production in the United States of the automotive product concerned produced by the firm, or an appropriate subdivision therefore, and of the automotive product like or directly competitive therewith, has decreased appreciably; and (3) (A) imports into the United States from Canada of the Canadian automotive product like or directly competitive with that produced by the firm, or an appropriate subdivision. thereof, have increased appreciably; or (B) exports from the United States to Canada . . . have decreased appreciably, and the decrease in such exports is greater than the decrease, if any, in production in Canada. . . ." If the three criteria are met, eligibility exists "unless . . . the Agreement has not been the *primary factor* in causing or threatening to cause (the) dislocation. . . ." If criteria (2) or (3) are not met, eligibility may exist if "the Agreement has nevertheless been the *primary factor* in causing or threatening to cause (the) dislocation."

Trade Act of 1974

Eligibility depends on a finding "(1) that a significant number or proportion of the workers in such workers' (impacted) firm or . . . subdivision have become totally or partially separated," or are threatened with such separation, "(2) that sales or production . . . of such firm or subdivision have decreased absolutely, and (3) that increases of imports of articles like or directly competitive with articles produced by such workers . . . *contributed importantly* to such total or partial separation, or threat . . . and to such decline in sales or production. . . . 'Contributed importantly' means a cause which is important but not necessarily more important than any other cause." Partial separation means a drop in average weekly hours and wages of 80 percent.

NOTE: Italics added for stress.

were not. When the union appealed to the courts, the Tariff Commission's ruling was upheld. The appeal was rejected on the basis of a legislative history of the phrase "like or directly competitive with" which predated the TEA. This phrase appeared in the Trade Agreements Extension Act of 1951 as part of an "escape clause." Escape clauses were introduced in the 1940s to provide semiautomatic tariff protection if an industry's claim of import injury was affirmed by a Tariff Commission investigation. Congress in 1955 had rejected an amendment that would have included components in the definition of "like or directly competitive with." Thus a piece of tariff legal history affected the administration of worker adjustment assistance.

The relation between escape-clause language and adjustment assistance language under the TEA is important. Drafters of the TEA included an escape clause (section 351) under which industries sometimes were able to obtain increased tariffs if they suffered injury. The injury was described in language very similar to that defining injury for purposes of adjustment assistance. During the 1940s and 1950s, escape clauses were interpreted very liberally and tended to upset trade agreements that the United States had previously negotiated. Since the TEA was a prelude to the Kennedy Round tariff negotiations, the intent of Congress was to restrict use of the escape clause to all but the most severe cases. But by using the same language for the escape clause and for adjustment assistance, the TEA's drafters presented the Tariff Commission with a difficult dilemma. The commission could not be liberal in approving adjustment assistance petitions without being liberal in approving escape-clause petitions. Thus, adjustment assistance—which was supposed to foster freer trade—was included in the TEA in such a way as to make its actual use inconsistent with that objective.

Criterion (3) illustrates the dilemma. The phrase "major factor" was included in the TEA's escape clause to make it much more restrictive than the escape clause in previous legislation. As a former chairman of the Tariff Commission has pointed out, the commission was bound to view the

43

language as requiring that increased imports be the most important causal factor in creating the injury.[15] Under this interpretation many petitions for adjustment assistance were dismissed because some other factor was found to be more important.

In any case, phrases like "the major factor" tend to be a lawyer's delight but an economist's nightmare. The commission dismissed several cases on the grounds that the workers concerned were primarily the victims of a change in consumer tastes or were employed by an inefficient plant. Unfortunately, it is very difficult to separate causal factors in such situations. Obviously, when an industry is under stress, the marginal firms and plants close. The cause of the particular firm or plant closure is always "marginality," due to such factors as inability to adapt to changes in consumer tastes or the possession of an antiquated and inefficient plant. Imports can be an important factor in determining how many marginal operations shut down or suffer injury. In escape-clause cases, the Tariff Commission was able to avoid such issues because it looked at an entire industry. But at the micro-level worker and firm cases under the TEA, the commission always was faced with factors other than imports which could account for injury of a particular unit.

The fourth criterion for general eligibility required that the injurious increase in imports be due to a trade *concession* "in major part." This requirement ensured limited applicability of adjustment assistance during the years immediately following the TEA's passage. The Kennedy Round resulted in major concessions, but negotiations were not completed until mid-1967 and cuts in tariffs did not begin to take effect until 1968. Hence, up until 1968, there had not been many major concessions. In a number of cases, petitions were dismissed because concessions had occurred only in the distant past, if at all. [16] In addition, in the interpretation of the Tariff Commission, unilateral tariff actions by the United States were not "concessions." Thus, imports entering under item 807.00 was not a concession in the context of a trade agreement. [17] (Items 806.30 and 807.00—discussed in Chapter 5—permit export and tariff-free reimport of U.S. products for foreign labor-intensive assembly operations.)

Finally, as in the cases of criteria (1) and (3), criterion (4) ran parallel to escape-clause language in the TEA, thus preventing the Tariff Commission from being liberal in one field without being liberal in the other.

The Automotive Products Trade Act solved the problem of the connection between the escape clause and adjustment assistance by removing the Tariff Commission from the determination of eligibility. Under the APTA, four criteria were set forth for the president to consider:[18] (1) whether dislocation of the workers had occurred or was threatening; (2) whether output of the product in the firm or subdivision had decreased, accompanied by a decrease in U.S. output of a product "like or directly competitive with" the firm or subdivision's product; (3) whether imports from Canada of a product "like or directly competitive with" the product made by the firm or subdivision had increased "appreciably"; (4) whether exports from the United States to Canada had decreased "appreciably," providing that the export decrease was less than the decrease, if any, which had occurred in Canadian production.

If criteria (1) and (2) and *either* of (3) or (4) were satisfied, eligibility was presumed to exist, unless the president determined that the U.S.-Canada automotive agreement was not the "primary factor" in causing or threatening to cause the dislocation. Even if criteria (2), (3), or (4) were not met, the president could certify eligibility if the agreement was nevertheless the "primary factor."

The APTA retained the "like or directly competitive" language of the TEA, but the problem of components was much less of an issue. Since the U.S.-Canada automotive agreement provided for free trade in new cars and *parts*, a reduction of automobile production in the United States need not have led to a reduction in orders for U.S.-made components. The parts could simply have been bought in the United States for use in Canadian production. Under APTA, a loss in *export* markets was compensable. Finally, rather than use the phrases "in major part" and "major factor," the APTA spoke of the "primary factor." "Primary factor" and "major factor" have essentially the same meaning.[19] But by using a different word and by removing the Tariff Commission, the APTA severed the link between the escape clause and adjustment assistance.

The decisions made by the president's delegates under the APTA were not as elegant as those of the Tariff Commission in terms of legal reasoning. But they provided aid. For example, the decisions sometimes specified that a certain percentage of the unemployment in a unit was due to the U.S.-Canada agreement and then arbitrarily allocated aid only to the workers involved. Out of twenty-one petitions for aid under the APTA, fourteen were approved, covering about 2,500 workers. About 1,950 workers actually received benefits totaling $4.1 million under the APTA, at a time when the TEA had provided no benefits whatsoever. [20] However, fewer than 100 workers received training. No petitions from firms were received under the APTA.

According to the Trade Act of 1974, the secretary of labor is to determine the eligibility of a worker unit on the basis of three criteria. These are: (1) that a significant number or proportion of the workers in the firm or subdivision have become, or are threatened with becoming "totally or partially separated"; (2) that sales and/or production of the firm or subdivision have decreased absolutely; (3) that increases of imports "like or directly competitive with" articles produced by the workers "contributed importantly" to the total or partial separation.

As approved by the Senate, the TA defined "contributed importantly" as "a cause which is important but not necessarily more important than any other cause." This specific definition was not included in the House-passed measure. In the final version the Senate provision was retained. Partial separation was defined as a reduction in average weekly hours and average weekly wages of 80 percent. The Senate-passed version of the TA required that the increase in imports under criterion (3) be "absolute," unlike the House bill. The final version removed the word "absolute," suggesting that a relative increase in the share of imports could satisfy criterion (3). Significantly, the TA does not require any linkage of the increase in imports to a trade concession.

The TA does contain escape-clause language, but adjustment assistance petitions are shielded from it in two ways. First, escape-clause investigations are handled by the Tariff Commission—now called the International Trade Commission—which has no responsibility for adjustment assistance investigations. Second, the language used in the escape clause is different from that in the adjustment assistance provisions. Increased imports have to be a "substantial cause" of injury under the escape clause, rather than an important contributor. A "substantial cause" is one "which is important and not less than any other cause." This differs from the adjustment assistance definition of "contributed importantly," which permits a qualifying cause to be less important than some other cause. Thus it is evident that access to adjustment assistance has been substantially eased.

Escape-clause language under the TA has been liberalized relative to the TEA as well and may lead to increased adjustment assistance for workers. Under the TEA, the president had the option of providing adjustment assistance as relief when the Tariff Commission ruled affirmatively (or split by tie vote) on an industry escape-clause petition. Under the TA, the International Trade Commission may recommend adjustment assistance as part of its remedy for escape-clause relief. Under such circumstances, the president can implement assistance through the secretary of labor (or commerce for firms). Only in these limited circumstances is there any involvement at all of the International Trade Commission or of the president in adjustment assistance. At this writing, there is no indication as to whether the commission will actively look into the potential usefulness of such assistance as part of its escape-clause investigations. While the commission is conducting its investigation, however, the secretary of labor is directed by the TA to prepare a study for the president. This study examines the number of workers in the industry who have been or are likely to be eligible for adjustment assistance and the availability of other existing programs that could facilitate adjustment.

Worker Eligibility and Benefits

Under the TEA and APTA, once a general determination of injury had been made, the Labor Department was responsible for providing a more specific description of the type of workers involved. Such a description—for example, workers who were laid off from division A of plant B after June 30, 1967—would enable local officials to process applications from impacted individuals. Such a procedure will continue under the new Trade Act of 1974. However, the general determination of injury and the determination of a specific description have been collapsed into a single Labor Department investigation.

To qualify for benefits, a worker in a certified unit had to meet two criteria. These are summarized in Table 3.3. The first was meant to establish general attachment to the labor force. The worker had to have been employed during 78 of the 156 weeks prior to the date of injury at a wage of at least $15 per week. A second criterion was intended to establish a linkage with the injured unit. The worker had to have been employed there for 26 of the 52 weeks at a wage of at least $15 per week prior to the injury date. In contrast, the TA removes the three-year work history requirement. Only 26 weeks of employment during the 52 weeks prior to injury at a wage of at least $30 per week in an impacted unit is required.

Under the TEA and APTA weekly benefits for unemployment or underemployment were set at 65 percent of the worker's average weekly wage, up to 65 percent of the national average weekly wage in manufacturing. In December 1974, when the TA was passed, average weekly earnings in manufacturing stood at about $185. The TA raised the cap from 65 to 100 percent—from $120 to $185—and raised the weekly benefit formula to 70 percent of the worker's average weekly wage. Thus a worker would not hit the cap unless his wage was about 42.9 percent above the national average $(1.00/.70 = 1.429)$. In December 1974, the cap would be effective at a weekly wage of about $264.

Both the TEA and APTA provided for a reduction in benefits if the worker had any earnings in a week of eligibility for assistance. Benefits were to be reduced by 50 percent of such

Table 3.3. Worker Adjustment Assistance Weekly Payments under Three Trade Acts

	Trade Expansion Act of 1962 and Automotive Products Trade Act of 1965	Trade Act of 1974
Qualifications	Just prior to date of injury employee must have (a) worked 78 of the last 156 weeks at wages of at least $15 per week, and (b) worked in a firm where worker injury occurred for 26 of the last 52 weeks at wages of at least $15 per week.	Just prior to date of injury employee must have been employed in a firm or subdivision where worker injury occurred for 26 of the last 52 weeks at wages of at least $30 per week.
Amount of weekly benefit *including normal unemployment compensation*	65 percent of worker's average weekly wage up to 65 percent of average weekly wage in U.S. manufacturing. State reimbursed for any unemployment insurance payments.	*70 percent* of worker's average weekly wage up to *100 percent* of average weekly wage in U.S. manufacturing. *Federal government pays only increment above state unemployment insurance.*
Provision for earnings during benefit period	Reduction of weekly benefit by 50 percent of earnings during week. Cap of 75 percent of worker's average weekly wage on income (earnings + benefits).	Reduction of weekly benefit by 50 percent of earnings during week. Cap of *80 percent* of worker's average weekly wage (*or, if less, 130 percent of U.S. average weekly manufacturing wage*).
Duration of payments	General case: up to 52 weeks.	General case: up to 52 weeks.
	Workers in training: up to 78 weeks.	Workers in training: up to 78 weeks.
	Workers aged 60 years and over: up to 65 weeks.	Workers aged 60 years and over: up to 78 weeks.

NOTE: Italics added for stress

earnings. This provision was carried over into the TA. However, the TEA and APTA both included an overall cap on the sum of worker earnings and benefits of 75 percent of his average weekly wage. The TA changed the cap to 80 percent, or 130 percent of the average national weekly manufacturing wage, whichever is less. The latter limit would affect only workers whose weekly income was more than 62.5 percent above the manufacturing wage $(1.30/.80 = 1.625)$.[21]

All three acts provided for a basic duration of weekly payments of 52 weeks, with an extension for workers undergoing training of 26 weeks. The TEA and APTA provided for a 13-week extension above the basic 52 weeks for workers aged sixty and over, in recognition of their greater mobility problems. This extension was raised to 26 weeks under the TA.

In addition to the weekly payments, the three acts provided other benefits meant to assist in readjustment to a new job. These are summarized in table 3.4. Workers were provided a subsistence allowance during training of $5 per day plus 10¢ per mile for transportation under the TEA and APTA. These amounts were raised to $15 per day and 12¢ per mile by the TA. All three laws provide for disqualification from the entire range of adjustment assistance benefits for failure to accept or to make satisfactory progress in suitable training.

Relocation was encouraged under all three acts if employment or an offer of employment was obtained at another location within the United States. The TEA and APTA limited the amount paid to two and a half times the average weekly wage in manufacturing ($463 in December 1974) plus moving expenses. Both laws limited eligibility to family heads. In contrast, the TA provided benefits to any injured workers and changed the lump-sum payment to three times the worker's weekly wage up to $500. Neither the TEA nor the APTA provided for job search allowances to encourage the worker to look outside of his immediate location for another job. The TA included an allowance for job searches within the U.S. of 80 percent of expenses up to a $500 cap. Job searches can be reimbursed only if there is no reasonable expectation of local employment.

50

Table 3.4. Worker Benefits Other Than Regular Weekly Payments under Three Trade Acts

	Trade Expansion Act of 1962 and Automotive Products Trade Act of 1965	*Trade Act of 1974*
Training	Workers may be given subsistence expense allowance of $5 per day and transportation expense allowance of 10¢ per mile while receiving training and related services.	If no suitable employment available, but employment would be available after training, secretary of labor may approve training, preferably on the job. Workers may be given subsistence expense allowance of *$15* and transportation allowance of *12¢* per mile. Worker who refused training without good cause is disqualified from all benefits.
Relocation qualifications	Family heads eligible if have obtained suitable employment or offer of employment with expectation of long-term duration within U.S.	*All* injured workers eligible if have obtained suitable employment or offer of employment with expectation of long-term duration within U.S.
Amount	Reasonable family moving and transportation expenses and a lump sum equal to 2 1/2 times U.S. average weekly manufacturing wage.	80 percent of reasonable family moving and transportation expenses and a lump sum equal to *3* times worker's average weekly wage, up to $500.
Job search	None	Allowance of 80 percent of job search expenses up to $500 for searches in U.S. of totally separated workers. Must be no reasonable expectation of finding local suitable employment.

NOTE: Italics added for stress.

The Statistical Record of Worker Adjustment Assistance

Table 3.5 presents a statistical summary of the case-processing record of the Tariff Commission through December 1974. About 48,000 workers were included in cases in which the

Table 3.5. Tariff Commission Determination on Worker Adjustment Assistance Petitions, Fiscal 1963-75

Fiscal year	Denied		Affirmed		Evenly Divided	
	Petitions	Workers	Petitions	Workers	Petitions	Workers
1963–1969	6	1,410	0	0	0	0
1970	2	700	6	2,012	5	1,100
1971	40	17,735	7	3,041	24	13,502
1972	41	16,125	9	6,815	0	0
1973	35	15,899	11	6,393	9	5,301
1974	24	7,034	8	2,630	3	1,260
First half 1975*	10	3,423	9	6,260	0	0
1963–1975†	158	62,326	50	27,151	41	21,163‡

SOURCE: Data supplied by U.S. Department of Labor.

*July 1974–December 1974.

†Through December 1974.

‡ Slight variations in estimated workers in this classification appear in Department of Labor documents.

commission made an affirmative finding of injury or was evenly divided. In the latter cases, the president followed a general policy of providing aid. All of the affirmative findings and evenly divided votes occurred after fiscal 1969.

A broad range of industries submitted petitions to the Tariff Commission, as can be seen in table 3.6. Not surprisingly, import-sensitive industries such as shoes, textiles, apparel, and electronics were among the petitioners. Out of 249 petitions to the Tariff Commission, only 50 received an affirmative decision (20 percent). Forty-one petitions ended with an even split among the commissioners. A smaller number of cases became eligible for worker adjustment assistance as the result of escape-clause industry petitions. Four industries, earthenware, marble, piano, and sheet glass, received affirmative escape-clause decisions. In accordance with TEA procedures, the Department of Labor

Table 3.6. Summary of U.S. Tariff Commission Determinations on Worker Adjustment Assistance Petitions by Industry, October 1962–December 1974

Industry	Denied Petitions	Denied Workers	Affirmed Petitions	Affirmed Workers	Evenly Divided* Petitions	Evenly Divided* Workers
Apparel						
Men's, youths' & boys' furnishings	2	325				
Men's, youths' & boys' suits	1	483				
Chemicals and allied products						
Synthetic fibers	1	1,000				
Dyes and pigments	1	500				
Electrical equipment						
Radio, TV, stereo, phonograph, and tape recorders	7	2,486	5	6,074	2	3,500
Electronic components	14	9,418	7	5,640	6	4,673
Electrical lighting and wiring equipment	3	650				
Food and kindred products						
Canned fruits & vegetables	1	200				
Fabricated metal products						
Structural metal products	1	288	3	450		
Leather products						
Men's shoes	15	4,040			1	230
Women's shoes	54	11,821	17	5,091	25	7,766
Shoe components	4	1,186				
Leather tanning	1	400				
Slippers	1	65				
Metal mining						
Iron ores	1	650				
Miscellaneous manufacturing industries						
Musical instruments			3	996	1	281
Games and toys	2	3,600				
Sporting goods	1	300				
Silverware and plated ware			3	1,820		
Nonelectrical machinery						
Metalworking machinery	2	2,200	1	26		
Office machines	2	2,500				
Nonmetalworking machinery	2	1,025				
General industrial machinery and equipment			1	650		

(Continued on next page)

Industry	Denied		Affirmed		Evenly Divided*	
	Peti-tions	Work-ers	Peti-tions	Work-ers	Peti-tions	Work-ers
Special industry machinery	1	340				
Primary metal industries						
Ferrous metal refining	5	1,695	1	400		
Nonferrous metal refining	2	530				
Rubber products						
Tires	1	100				
Rubber footwear	3	1,830	2	1,162	4	4,070
Misc. rubber products	2	1,550				
Stone, clay and glass products						
Structural clay products	3	802				
Glass products	3	455				
Pottery products	1	290				
Cut stone and stone products			1	100		
Textile mill products						
Cotton fabrics	6	2,410	5	2,742	1	93
Knitted fabrics	3	3,000				
Manmade fabrics	1	600				
Wool fabrics	4	1,347				
Spun yarn	2	1,600				
Yarn and thread	1	1,700				
Misc. textile products	1	165				
Transportation equipment						
Motor vehicles			1	2,000		
Motor vehicle parts	2	545			1	150
Motorcycles, bicycles, & parts	1	230				
Totals	158	62,326	50	27,151	41	20,763†

SOURCE: Data supplied by U.S. Department of Labor.
*When the commission is evenly divided and makes no finding, the president under Section 330(d) (1) of the Tariff Act of 1930, as amended, may accept either view of the commissioners as the finding of the commission. Numbers of workers are estimated.
†Slight variations in estimated workers in this classification appear in Department of Labor documents.

considered petitions for aid from worker units in firms operating within these four industries. Fifteen such petitions, involving about 4,100 workers, received affirmative decisions from the Labor Department. Although the largest number of petitions and workers came from Massachusetts—an important shoe producer—the state distribution of petitions and certified workers was scattered broadly. Thirty-one states were involved in the servicing of trade-injured workers, so local authorities across the country have had some experience in the administrative aspects of the adjustment assistance program. In many jurisdictions, however, the experience has been extremely limited.

Neither the state authorities nor the Labor Department has maintained a detailed record system on the individuals certified for aid. Two doctoral dissertations on the subject of adjustment assistance have made use of sample data to evaluate the program. The first study, by Malcolm D. Bale, relied on a hurriedly gathered sample of workers from trade-impacted units taken by the Labor Department in 1972.[22] The sample involved over four hundred workers in twelve cases covering a variety of industries. A second study by James E. McCarthy relied on a sample drawn by the author exclusively from the shoe industry in Massachusetts.[23]

Labor Department officials tend to be suspicious of the quality of the Bale data because the survey method depended on worker recollections rather than verifiable records. A subsequent spot check of the accuracy of these recollections against program records suggested that the responses often were faulty. The McCarthy survey does not suffer from this problem, but its limited industry and geographic scope leave something to be desired in terms of an overall picture of the program. However, as table 3.7 shows, both samples have certain common characteristics.

The Bale and McCarthy samples both indicate that trade-impacted workers tend to be older individuals, employed at relatively low-wage jobs. There tend to be more females than in the national work force as a whole, with characteristics that suggest limited potential mobility. For example, they had been

Table 3.7.   Characteristics of Samples from Two Studies

Bale sample		McCarthy sample	
Mean age	44 years	Mean age	53.7 years
White-Anglo Saxon	91%	White–U.S. born	85.7%
Female	49%	Female	71.0%
Mean educational attainment	8–9 years	Mean educational attainment	9.0 years
Mean hourly wage before displacement	$3.02	Mean weekly wage before displacement	$100.40
Shoe workers	$2.84		
Textile workers	$2.56		
Other workers	$3.56		
		Always lived within 100 miles of birth-place	73.8%
		Skills specific to shoe industry	48.5%
Mean length of service with impacted firm		Mean length of service with impacted firm	12.9 years
Shoe workers	7.8 years		
Textile workers	10.1 years		
Other workers	10.7 years		
		Mean length of service in shoe industry	26.1 years
Size of initial sample	424	Size of initial sample	200
Number of Cases*	12	Number of Cases*	12

*The two studies included one case in common.

on their original jobs for a significant period of time. And, in the case of the McCarthy sample, almost three-fourths of the workers had always lived within one hundred miles of their birthplaces. Educational attainment averaged considerably less than completion of high school. Relatively few of the workers in either study belonged to racial minorities. In the McCarthy sample, "minorities" consisted largely of white immigrants from eastern and southern Europe. Minorities in the Bale survey were mainly Mexican-Americans.

Both Bale and McCarthy used multiple regression to determine what factors "explained" differences in the labor-force experiences of workers injured due to imports. Bale was interested in determining factors associated with improvement or deterioration in a worker's wages from the period prior to the import impact to the current job. He also focused on the absolute wage received currently and on the number and proportion of days after layoff during which the worker was unemployed. McCarthy also was interested in the wage impact, although he distinguished between the wage change from layoff to the next job and from layoff to the current job. In addition, McCarthy looked at the number of weeks unemployed between layoff and the next job and the number of weeks of TEA and unemployment insurance benefits collected.

Details of the results of these investigations are best obtained from the primary sources themselves. However, a number of the findings are especially interesting. Male workers and primary family wage earners (the two are highly correlated) seemed to fare better after layoff than females and secondary workers. Presumably, this is at least partially a reflection of greater pressure on primary breadwinners to obtain new employment. Age seemed to be a helpful factor, too, although at a diminishing rate in the older years. On the other hand, high unemployment rates in the local labor market tended to prolong the period of joblessness for trade-impacted workers.

A problem with statistical techniques of the type used by McCarthy and Bale is that they do not reveal the structural mechanisms that underlie the correlations. Many factors are at work, and some push in opposing directions. The correlation technique simply reveals the *net* effect. In some cases, this produces anomalous results. For example, Bale found that workers who used the employment service for training and testing fared worse than those who did not. Critics of the employment service may take heart from this perverse correlation. But it probably means only that when workers found themselves unable to deal with their problem on their own, they looked to the employment service for assistance.

One of the most interesting findings in the Bale dissertation concerns the length of time required to obtain assistance under the TEA program. Bale found a mean waiting time from separation to first TEA payment of almost fifty-five weeks, a duration longer than the basic payment period for adjustment assistance (table 3.8). This delay meant that many workers received their payments in a lump sum, after their spell of unemployment, and that they did not need training and relocation. Many workers had already made their adaptation prior to receiving assistance. Moreover, it is doubtful that the mere possibility of eventually receiving aid helped workers to deal with displacement. Bale found that most workers had only a hazy idea about the types of benefits available to them.

Table 3.8.   Average Time Periods Required for Processing Adjustment Assistance under the TEA

	Period	Weeks
(1)	Impact date to separation	18.2
(2)	Separation to unit certification	32.7
(3)	Certification to individual application	14.9
(4)	Application and first TEA payment	6.9
	Separation to first TEA payment Sum of (2) (3) (4)	54.5
(5)	Separation to first UI payment	7.4
(6)	Application to first UI payment	2.1

SOURCE: Statement of Malcolm D. Bale in U.S. House, Committee on Ways and Means, *Trade Reform* (Washington, D.C.: U.S. Government Printing Office, 1973), p. 1192. Data also appear in Malcolm D. Bale, "Adjustment to Freer Trade: An Analysis of the Adjustment Assistance Provisions of the Trade Expansion Act of 1962" (Ph.D. diss., University of Wisconsin-Madison, 1973), p. 137.

Problems in TEA Administration

Discussions of the problems in the TEA's adjustment assistance program usually revolve around bureaucratic procedures and eligibility rules. The latter issue has already been mentioned and the former will be treated below. However, the program seems to have suffered from a more fundamental flaw: the lack of a clear-cut political base.

Under the TEA, workers who were injured by import concessions were singled out for special benefits and were to be treated differently from workers injured by automation, vagaries in demand, and the myriad other causes of layoffs and displacements. The official rationale for this special treatment was always that TEA-type injuries resulted from a government policy change and the persons should receive government compensation. The actual rationale, however, seemed to revolve around the political question of obtaining labor support for passage of the TEA.

Once the TEA was passed, interest in the actual operation of the program diminished, not to arise again until a new trade bill was under consideration. There might have been internal support from the government bureaucracy if the program had amounted to anything in its early years. The Labor Department initially prepared itself for a considerable volume of cases, but when it became apparent that Tariff Commission approval was difficult to obtain, government interest in the program also diminished. The only possible remaining constituency was the unions in import-sensitive industries, but these saw adjustment assistance as largely a post-mortem operation. Unions in import-sensitive industries were naturally more concerned with obtaining trade restrictions than with adjustment assistance.

If any significant group had been actively involved in the adjustment assistance program, Congress probably would have modified it as soon as its problems became evident. Congress did establish a special adjustment program for the automobile workers affected by the U.S.-Canada automotive agreement. No such moves, however, were made on behalf of workers covered by the TEA adjustment provisions.

Delays in processing petitions were built into the program—perhaps inadvertently—by Congress. A number of levels and agencies of government were involved in administration, an almost sure-fire guarantee of a slow operation. The Tariff Commission suddenly was saddled with a program involving investigations at the firm or plant level. This represented a deviation from its usual industry investigations for which a trade association with reasonable resources was available to support petitions and supply data. But the commission staff found that adjustment assistance petitioners often lacked the data—particularly with regard to imports and sales—necessary for a report to the commissioners. Employers were not always willing to take on the burden of supplying information, particularly if they were undergoing bankruptcy. The small enterprises that often were involved sometimes did not have the needed data. The situation was not helped by the lack of an application form for petitioners until late in 1972.

Union officials, despite complaints over Tariff Commission procedures, sometimes were slow about filing petitions. They saw the aid that might be received as "burial insurance." [24] Workers received their regular unemployment insurance payments promptly anyway, and any TEA payments would be simply an increment to these. Thus some union officials did not file petitions on an urgent basis. Nonunion workers were unlikely to know about the existence of the TEA program.

Occasionally a letter from a nonunion worker or a union worker (whose union had not filed a petition) would reach the Labor Department, usually a request for help in a layoff situation without reference to TEA payments or assistance. If imports seemed to be involved, the letter would be routed to the appropriate department officials, who would assist in developing the necessary petition.

With some exceptions in the shoe industry, the department did not actively seek petitions. More activity might have been stimulated through a public relations campaign. For example, posters concerning the program could have been placed in local employment service offices, but since Tariff Commission approval was uncertain, such a campaign might simply have led to unrealistic expectations by petitioners. Once it became clear that the program would be limited, only a small staff was allocated to it in the Department of Labor.

The Tariff Commission had a statutory sixty days to process petitions, but since adequate data were often not included in initial petitions, the commission would refuse to accept the submission until it was relatively complete. In some instances, weeks and even months passed before the sixty-day "clock" was activated.

In the number of the cases that resulted in evenly divided votes at the Tariff Commission, the final injury decision was left to the president. Given the general White House disposition to approve such cases, it might have been expected that presidential processing would have been expedited, but the Office of the Special Trade Representative, which handled the White House operation, did not always place high priority on rapid processing.

Cases with affirmative decisions eventually were returned to the Labor Department for a certification investigation. This meant that department investigators would have to go back over some of the ground already covered by Tariff Commission officials. In addition, the department investigators would have to determine which subset of workers in a group were injured by imports rather than by other causes. Since persons often worked on several products—only one of which might have been covered by the original petition—these decisions sometimes were arbitrary.

As the investigation proceeded, the Manpower Administration would inform state unemployment and employment service authorities about the potential workload involved. Most states had only a handful of cases under TEA. Few state officials were aware of the program's existence. Usually, the Manpower Administration maintained a limited contact with the few people at the state level who had been assigned responsibility. (This selection was generally on an informal and ad hoc basis.) These state representatives would inform whatever local offices were to be involved, then instruction concerning application forms and the like was provided to the local offices.

Local authorities probably viewed the TEA program as a minor annoyance perpetrated from on high. Compared with the normal unemployment insurance and employment service workload, the TEA program was tiny, but it required a deviation from normal routines. The forms and the nature of information needed to determine eligibility for TEA payments were different from those needed for unemployment insurance purposes. Three-year work histories had to be obtained. Employer records often were not immediately forthcoming. The long lag in reaching the local office meant that some workers were no longer easily located. In short, TEA was likely to be an administrative nuisance, and since so much time already had elapsed, and the payments were often retroactive, there might be little sense of urgency.

The TEA stated that workers would be eligible for "testing, counseling, training, and placement services provided for under any Federal law," but the meaning was not clear. Such services to trade-impacted workers were provided through the local employment service office, but were available to *any* worker, not just those falling under the TEA program. Indeed, since trade-impacted workers received ordinary unemployment compensation before TEA allowances, they probably had been channeled to the employment service prior to TEA certification.

One interpretation of the TEA's provision for special services is that trade-impacted workers would get priority. That is, if a single training slot was available, a trade-impacted worker might receive it in preference to an otherwise identical applicant [25] There is some doubt, however, as to whether a local employment service office would operate in that fashion. In some cases, trade-impacted workers received private training, with the costs reimbursed under TEA. The degree to which this occurred was probably a function of worker initiative and/or the initiative of particular local officials.

It is not surprising to find that the TEA program generally failed to provide much assistance in facilitating *adjustment*. To the extent that a congressional intent on the operation of the program can be perceived, adjustment rather than lump-sum payments probably would have been preferred. However, the main purpose of the program appears to have been to obtain passage of a trade bill. Thus, as has been noted, no modifications were made until 1974, when a new trade bill was passed. Prospects under the new legislation for improved worker adjustment assistance are the subject of Chapter 4.

4

Manpower Implications
of Worker Adjustment Assistance: Future Prospects

Administrative and Budgetary Considerations

The key aspects of the new worker adjustment assistance program included in the Trade Act of 1974 are (1) improved benefits, (2) less stringent rules for unit eligibility, and (3) new administrative arrangements for processing petitions. The last is important, since the Department of Labor can be expected to take a "friendlier" attitude toward applications. In addition, processing time can be reduced since the initial determination of eligibility and the certification investigation have been collapsed into a single review. No White House involvement is needed except in escape-clause cases.

All these features tend to make the new program more attractive to potential applicant units. The cost of applying will not be great; the Labor Department will do most of the necessary fact-finding. Thus an increase in applications may be expected. In response to this caseload potential, the International Labor Affairs Bureau was granted forty-five additional staff members. The key questions are (1) Will the additional resources be sufficient given the structure of the program? and (2) Is the program properly designed to meet its objectives?

Resources

The additional staff resources are not likely to be underemployed. By taking a more active posture than it had under TEA, the Department of Labor could always generate sufficient business to keep its personnel fully occupied. The program case load might exceed Labor Department expectations, however, particularly in periods of relatively high general unemployment. Why should not a unit of workers faced with unemployment—particularly a unionized unit—risk the price of a first-class letter to ask for a determination? There is always the chance that the Labor Department might find that imports have "contributed importantly" to their situation.

With the requirement removed that an import *concession* be shown as the key determinant, workers in many manufacturing industries might make some sort of case for consideration. Areas that hitherto have not generated cases may now begin to submit petitions. For example, regions in the southwestern states were not able to petition for relief from imports from the Mexican Border Development Program under the old TEA provisions because the Tariff Commission did not consider items 806.30 and 807.00 of the Tariff Schedules—on which the Development Program depends—to be "concessions." But this ruling has no relevance to the new TA program.

The Tariff Commission spent about one-half to two-thirds of a man-year on a TEA worker adjustment investigation and report. This estimate includes clerical, legal, and editorial time as well as actual field work. Some Labor Department officials believe they can reduce substantially the time required for an investigation and point to their previous experience on escape-clause investigations. If the Labor Department could reduce the resource requirements to one-fourth of a man-year, the 45 additional staff members could process 180 cases. The average case size under the old TEA program was about 443 workers per case. If this average size continued, 180 cases suggest about 80,000 workers.

While the Trade Act was being considered in Congress, an estimate of one hundred thousand workers receiving payments each year came into vogue. The empirical foundation for this estimate is unclear. If it proves to be accurate, it would imply a still higher number of workers in initial petitions since some applications presumably would be denied. In addition, not all certified workers actually receive payments. Some workers find new jobs immediately, retire, or do not collect benefits for other reasons. In short, even assuming that planned Labor Department staff could handle petitions resulting in aid to one hundred thousand workers, departmental resources could be overstretched by still larger numbers. Of course, the future workload can not be forecast with any accuracy. Much will depend on the record of "generosity" established by the Labor Department and the pressure the department may feel to solicit petitions actively.

Various estimates of the costs of the new program have been made. One of these, based on an internal Labor Department document, is reproduced in table 4.1. This estimate is based on the assumption of one hundred thousand workers receiving benefits per year. It assumes that the weekly allowances would cost over $480 million during the first full year of operation. This comes to about 90 percent of the total budget. Less than 3 percent of the budget is for state and federal administrative expenses. The rest goes for training, job search, and relocation allowances. The total amount of the budget, over $.5 billion, is higher than some earlier private estimates.[1]

The federal costs of the program, as it finally emerged in the Trade Act, will be considerably less because, unlike the TEA provisions, the TA does not provide for federal reimbursement of state unemployment insurance payments. State unemployment payments follow a variety of formulas that make it difficult to determine how much of the benefit expenditure comes from state budgets. The standard state duration of benefits is 26 weeks, although some states have longer periods. Twenty-six weeks is just half of the basic 52 weeks permitted under the TA program. During periods of high unemployment, Congress often provides for longer durations, as was done in late 1974. Benefits under state programs generally cluster between 50 to 60 percent of weekly earnings, significantly below the 70

Table 4.1. Budget Estimate for Workers' Adjustment Under Trade Act of 1974, First Full Year

	Estimated number of workers	Average benefit per week	Average duration in weeks	Cost
Unemployment Allowance				
Workers under age 60	91,500	$133	34.0	$413,800,000
Workers over age 60	8,500	$133	61.0	69,000,000
Job search allowance	6,000*			3,000,000
Relocation allowance	2,000†			2,400,000
Training grants	24,300‡			31,590,000
State administrative expenses incidental to allowances				8,000,000
State administrative expenses incidental to employment services				4,170,000
Federal administration				2,863,000
Total allowances and administration				$534,823,000

SOURCE: Internal Department of Labor Memorandum.
*Estimated average payment of $500.
†Estimated average payment of $1,200.
‡Estimated average payment of $1,300.

percent permitted under the TA's adjustment provisions, and they often include caps on benefits. Charging the normal unemployment benefits against the state programs might reduce the cost of the allowances to the federal government in some years by as much as 75 percent.[2] This would cut the overall federal cost of the program by about two-thirds.

The original $.5 billion estimate is of interest, even though it may be inaccurate, as a crude estimate of adjustment costs of international trade. Since some of the projected hundred thousand workers would have become unemployed anyway over the course of a year due to nonimport factors, the $.5 billion overestimates the cost. The degree to which involuntary unemployment would otherwise affect trade-sensitive workers is difficult to estimate. However, the adjustment for this factor is relatively small, compared with the magnitude and crudity of the original estimate. Thus Congress likely will look at the costs of the TA program calculated on a basis similar to that given in table 4.1 when considering the trade-off between adjustment assistance and import restrictions.

Program Design

The principle of adjustment assistance could be defended in a variety of ways. It could be regarded primarily as a form of monetary compensation for injuries suffered by a particular group of workers on behalf of a greater "social" interest in promoting freer trade. Two factors, however, suggest that this rationale was not the chief motivation of Congress in passing the program. First, to be totally compensatory, adjustment assistance would have to offer benefits high enough so that the workers involved would have been indifferent between retaining their jobs or losing them and obtaining adjustment payments. The original TEA program was somewhat closer to the "payoff" model since it won the support of organized labor—the presumed representatives of the potentially injured workers—for trade expansion. But the revised program in 1974 did not win labor's endorsement, even though the benefits were made more generous. Thus, as has been stated in the previous chapter, the adjustment assistance program is better viewed as a method of obtaining support (or reduced resistance) for a trade bill than as a direct attempt to compensate injured workers for 100 percent of their injuries.

Second, trade adjustment assistance includes features that would not be contained in a simple compensation scheme. It provides for training and for job search and moving allowances, all of which suggest an intent to subsidize a smoother transition from job to job. Presumably, if the motivation for the program had been only compensation, flat cash grants—with no strings attached—would have been the appropriate form of benefit. Recipients would have been free to use their payments to purchase training, finance job searches, or pay moving expenses, but only if they so desired. The fact that categorical grants were made suggests a different, paternal motivation. Congress wished to make sure that the payments were used for the "right" purposes.

Social welfare programs with an employment orientation are certainly not the exclusive property of the adjustment assistance program. The United States has subsidized the obtaining of manpower services for many years, reaching back to the 1920s for vocational education and the 1930s for the employment service. However, a special interest in manpower programs developed in the early 1960s.[3] It is no accident that import adjustment assistance developed at approximately the same time that Congress passed the Area Redevelopment Act and the Manpower Development and Training Act (MDTA).

Many manpower programs were spawned under the legislation of the 1960s. Still more are being operated today under the Comprehensive Employment and Training Act of 1973 (CETA), which replaced most of the older programs. Although a multiplicity of programs has developed, they usually are more general than the TEA or TA program. A manpower program may well be tailored to serve a specific target group, which certainly is a reasonable purpose. The target groups usually were designated on the basis of income level, ethnic origin, or location, with the presumption that individuals within the target group would possess sufficient similarities of "need" so that their problems could be handled uniformly. In contrast, the TEA and the TA were based on similarity of source of injury, not similarity of need.

The design of the TEA and TA programs can be understood easily in terms of the political process that produced them. But this process did not take much account of rational program design. Injury by imports does not produce a sufficiently homogeneous population around which a manpower program otherwise would be structured. No evidence has yet been adduced that a worker displaced by imports is significantly different from a worker displaced by changing technology, declining demand, or other common causes of unemployment. In contrast, there may be sufficient commonality surrounding such groups as young unemployed veterans just out of the service, or unemployed ghetto teenagers, to justify the MDTA or CETA programs created for them.

In some respects, however, the clientele of the import adjustment assistance program may be more amenable to a statistical "success" than many of the target groups selected for other programs since the 1960s. The manpower programs of the 1960s often were "sold" as macro policy instruments. First, they would solve an impending structural crisis.[4] Then they would shift the U.S. Phillips curve and make price stability and low unemployment feasible.[5] Finally, they would eliminate poverty. Automation jitters quickly subsided as the economy expanded. But the problem of inflation grew. So did interest in poverty issues, thanks to the civil rights movement and the Johnson administration's War on Poverty. Charged with resolving major social dilemmas, manpower administrators were encouraged to seek out clients with the most intractable problems and were criticized for "creaming" the unemployed if they chose workers most likely to be helped.[6]

The fact is that workers displaced by imports are more likely to have the characteristics for which manpower programs were originally designed in the early 1960s. They are likely to be factory workers, often semiskilled or even skilled, who have had considerable work experience. Their job skills may need some adjustment, but in most cases, they will not lack basic social skills such as literacy or work orientations. In a sense, the adjustment program will be creaming the unemployed, the very sin other programs are not supposed to commit.

By the late 1960s, manpower programs often concentrated their efforts in what has been termed the "secondary" labor market, with its low wages, high turnover, lack of unionization, and lack of coverage by social welfare legislation. A number of the industries that have been affected by imports—such as shoes and electronics—have tended to be lower-wage sectors. But with the broader definitions of eligibility in the TA program, workers in a substantially wider area in manufacturing are likely to be adjustment assistance recipients. Industries such as automobiles, steel, and tires might well produce TA cases. Moreover, there is a tendency—especially if the Labor Department does not play an active role in soliciting applications—for petitions to come from unionized workers. Unions are more likely to be aware of the benefits of the program than groups of unorganized workers.

Some critics might argue that the resources that will be spent on the TA program "ought" to be applied to more needy unemployed workers, that resources will be misallocated by giving special attention to displaced workers who happen to be import-injured. But whatever the merits of the debate on need versus cause of injury, it is not a live issue to Congress. The TA program probably will remain unchanged for many years, as long as its administrators do not prove to be too tightfisted. The administrators of TA are in an enviable position relative to the operators of other manpower programs. Their program is not likely to be the victim of an administrative shuffle or the changing moods regarding federal versus local control. And it has the specific backing of Congress.

Aside from direct cash payments, the new TA program offers three features specifically aimed at easing the transition to new employment: training, job search allowance, and relocation benefits. The TA does not itself establish a mechanism for training. It, in effect, leaves the decision on training to the client and his employment service counselor. Training presumably will take place in facilities already available in the community. Public training efforts are now mainly operated locally under grants from the federal government under the Comprehensive Employment and Training Act. It is unclear that the operators of such local programs would give priority to import-injured workers in filling available training slots, but they may find the prospect of federally funded tuition inviting. The worker might also find a private training facility and convince the employment service counselor to provide the necessary funding.

The TA specifically suggests that training should be on the job, but past experience has not proved that a priori preference should be given to on-the-job-training over institutional programs. Observed costs per trainee are often lower in on-the-job-training programs, but it is not always clear that employers have been stimulated to provide more training than they otherwise would have.[7] Of course, from the viewpoint of the import-injured client, such considerations are unimportant. Even if an employer does not provide extra training, he still will be encouraged to give preference in hiring to import-injured candidates over others since these applicants come with a subsidy.

Under the TA, a job search allowance of 80 percent of costs (up to $500) is provided for searches away from the worker's home area. Presumably the client would have to convince his employment service counselor in advance that the area of the proposed search was likely to produce employment. There is no way of predicting the success rates that might be expected from such job searches. Most studies find that job searches are made through informal channels such as information obtained from friends and relatives.[8] If a candidate had contacts in the search area, therefore, he would be more likely to be successful than if he simply checked in at the local employment service office.

Some evidence on relocation allowances is available from experimental programs operated under the MDTA.[9] In some cases, high rates of return to the original home area were experienced several months after relocation. The problem often appeared to be a form of culture shock affecting disadvantaged rural persons who suddenly found themselves in a large city. Under the TA, as noted earlier, the clientele need not be disadvantaged, and the relocations need not involve a change in the type of area of residence.

The relocation benefit under the old TEA was moving expenses plus a lump-sum payment of two and a half times the average weekly wage in manufacturing. At the time the new bill was passed, the lump sum would have been about $463. Under the TA, only 80 percent of moving expenses will be paid, and the lump sum was set equal to three times the *worker's* weekly wage up to $500. Although some workers conceivably could qualify for more under the new program (the difference between $500 and $463 might outweigh the unfunded 20 percent of moving expenses), most would get less. The loss is somewhat illusionary, however, since practically no relocation payments were made under the TEA.

Relocation costs could vary considerably depending on distance and the number of family members involved. The combination of variable payment for moving expenses plus lump sum provides some incentive to minimize expenses, since 20 percent of moving costs must be paid by the worker. If the move were short and the family small, the worker might come out "ahead" in some circumstances because of the lump-sum payment. There is clearly a strong financial incentive for clients to consider the *possibility* of moving, particularly if local job-seeking efforts have proved unsuccessful. However, neither the job search allowance nor the relocation benefit would have any impact unless the previous delays in processing adjustment assistance applications are reduced under the new program. If eligibility is not determined until after the worker has made his adjustment—as was often the case under TEA—the job-seeking incentive effects will be lost.

Complementary Trade Programs

Although the bulk of attention under the new Trade Act's adjustment provisions undoubtedly will center on worker cases, the act does provide assistance to firms and communities. McCarthy, in his study of the Massachusetts shoe industry, discussed in Chapter 3, concluded that firm assistance indirectly benefited workers. [10] Firms are eligible to receive loans, loan guarantees, and technical assistance through the secretary of commerce if they meet the act's criteria for import injury. In addition, unlike the old TEA, communities are now eligible for assistance in the form of loans and loan guarantees to attract new investment. This program also could have an indirect effect on workers. Firms that receive loans through a community program are mildly encouraged to establish an employee stock ownership plan. [11] More important, the development of new industry in a trade-impacted area would help workers find new jobs in their communities, thus alleviating the pressure for substantial mobility.

The Trade Act establishes an Adjustment Assistance Coordinating Committee with representatives from the Office of the Special Trade Representative, the Small Business Administration, and the Labor and Commerce Departments. The committee is charged with coordination of adjustment assistance programs. In addition, the General Accounting Office is directed to make a study prior to the termination date of the adjustment programs, reviewing their effectiveness. Program operation and review are to be fostered by a new trade statistics monitoring system to be developed at the Departments of Labor and Commerce.[12] The intent is to relate imports to employment and production.

Firms are directed to provide sixty days' notice to their employees and to the Departments of Labor and Commerce before transferring facilities abroad.[13] A mechanism for enforcement of this provision is not included in the act. Congress expresses its "sense" that such firms should apply for adjustment assistance (presumably this means cooperation with worker and/or community petitions), should offer alternative employment opportunities in the U.S. to its workers—if any exist—and should assist its employees in relocation. What effect this notice and other requirements may have is unclear; however, advance notice may shorten the delay between separation and adjustment assistance for some workers.

Final Throughts on Adjustment Assistance

The import adjustment assistance program raises some important questions for manpower policy. In many respects, the adjustment assistance program never has been taken seriously in its own right. Adjustment assistance has been primarily a device to pass trade bills, a function it helped to perform on two occasions.[14] The original rationale was that the government should help individuals who were hurt by government actions such as tariff concessions. With the "concession" requirement removed from the TA, the basis for singling out imports as a source of injury as opposed to technical change, decreases in demand, and others is unclear. One might argue that all sources of injury should be compensated at TA rates; adjustment assistance could be viewed as a "foot in the door" for an eventual all-injury program. But this approach again involves a political calculation rather than a specific justification for import assistance.

Many programs are inconsistent when judged on a "needs" basis. A seventy-year-old is eligible for Medicare; a forty-year-old with an identical medical problem is not. In most states, a worker disabled on the job is eligible for workers' compensation; a worker disabled at home is not.[15] In many of these examples special circumstances explain the inconsistency. Medicare is aimed at older individuals because medical costs rise with age, *on average*. Workers' compensation arose out of inadequacy of the court system to deal with employer liability for worker injury. Other programs have significant constituent backing, and their outcomes are taken seriously by their supporters. This support has never characterized import adjustment assistance. Congress is not going to worry much about the manpower implications of a program whose main purpose is to pass trade bills.

The new TA program probably will not bring about any fundamental change, though it will be more liberal, and more money will be handed out to more people. In that sense, the program will be more successful as a provider of "compensation." As *adjustment* assistance, it is not clear that the new program will be more effective than the old. Attention is more likely to focus on the number of workers aided rather than on the effects of the aid. Overall success depends on the administrators of the program, who need to develop a natural constituency. Organized labor at the national level cannot be publicly enthusiastic about adjustment assistance, since it prefers to concentrate on changing U.S. trade policy. The unions most immediately involved are left in the ambiguous position of dealing with a program whose avowed purpose is to help their members find work elsewhere—often outside their jurisdiction. Thus, if any change is to occur in the adjustment process, the Department of Labor must act as its own prod.

5

Labor Issues Surrounding the Multinational Firm

General Background

If "multinational firm" is defined as a firm that operates in more than one country, the institution is not new. The Hudson's Bay Company (established 1670) and the Dutch West India Company (established 1621) can be considered early prototypes. What is new is the concern about multinationals, which in recent years has produced a flood of printed matter.

Before the impact on labor of multinationals can be considered, we must determine how "important" they are to the economy. In certain respects, the answer seems obvious. Tabulations such as table 5.1 show that U.S.-based multinational firms have expanded their overseas investment substantially in the postwar period. Foreign-based direct investment in the United States also has expanded rapidly, although in absolute terms it has been much smaller than the reverse flow. At one level, therefore, an institution involving such large dollar magnitudes is definitely "important."

The key question about multinationals is whether there are substitutes for them. If multinationals did not exist, in other words, how different would world trade and investment be? The answer is not obvious. Multinationals are not the only channel

Table 5.1.   Direct Investment in the U.S. and Abroad, 1950–1974 ($ billions)

	By US firms abroad		By foreign firms in the US	
	1950	1974	1950	1974
Canada	3.6	28.4	1.0	4.8
Europe	1.7	44.5	2.2	14.1
Japan	*	3.3		.5
Latin America and other western hemisphere except Canada	4.6	19.6	.1	.5
Other†	1.9	22.8		1.8
Manufacturing	3.8	50.9	1.1	10.3
Petroleum	3.4	30.2	.4	5.9
Other	4.6	37.4	1.9	5.5
Total	$11.8	$118.6	$3.4	$21.7

SOURCE: Department of Commerce, various studies.
*Less than $.05 billion.
†Includes shipping companies using flags of convenience in Panama and Liberia.

for international investment flows. In 1974, of the $31.7 billion in net private capital outflows from the United States, only $7.3 billion took the form of direct investment, that is, investment via multinationals. Similarly, of the $21.7 billion of net capital inflows from abroad, only $2.2 billion represented direct investment by foreigners. In short, international investment flows take place through many channels—bank loans, purchases of securities, extension of trade credits, and the like—not just through equity transactions involving multinational firms.

If investment can flow through various channels, so can trade. A special study by the Tariff Commission found that 31 percent of U.S. exports were conducted by multinationals in 1970 and 27.5 percent of imports.[1] Most trade, therefore, is not simply an internal transaction of a multinational enterprise, and the figures would be significantly lower if trade with Canada—where many U.S.-based firms operate—was omitted.

The two other areas often associated with multinationals are transfers of technology and transfers of managerial skills. No figures are available that break down the multinational components of such transactions. Both types of transactions can occur without being internal to a single firm. Firms can sell patent rights and license technology to other firms, and, of course, management consulting skills can be bought and sold through interfirm transactions.

Most economists would argue that the primary forces determining flows of capital, goods, technology, and management skills are cost considerations. Funds are borrowed where interest rates are lower. Goods are imported from countries where their costs of production are lower. Even technology and management skills can be viewed as originating in areas where there is a comparative advantage in their production.

The logic of this argument is that even if multinationals did not exist, some other substitute channels would be found to perform the same function. Although the factors involved are not well understood, multinationals themselves presumably exist because of comparative advantages inherent to that form of organization. Perhaps multinationals—by operating in many countries—gain an advantage over purely national firms in terms of the availability of knowledge. They are better able to perceive cost advantages around the world and therefore to exploit them more fully than could a national firm.

Multinationals have a bigger impact through the political arena. Leftists—particularly in less-developed countries—have considered multinationals capitalist exploiters, that receive support from their home governments in their pursuit of corporate profits; in some cases they are right. At a more mundane level, however, it seems clear that the increased importance of multinationals has had a political impact on American trade policy. Multinationals have become an important domestic interest group with a self-interest in freer trade. In recent years, they have been able to overcome the traditional local forces favoring protection. The Trade Act of 1974 is in no small measure a tribute to this realignment of political influence. And since government trade policy can affect labor, multinationals certainly have had an impact through the political channel.

77

Impact on Labor

Chapter 1 pointed to two types of impacts that trade could have on labor. First, it could lead to changes in the domestic pattern of production—the factor-supply explanation of trade—which in turn could have a long-run effect on real wages. An argument for multinationals is that if they do have a special advantage in conducting trade, the volume of trade in both directions is somewhat larger than it otherwise might be. In turn, the existence of multinationals might give trade a greater impact on real wages in the long run. This line of reasoning is highly speculative.[2]

A second area of interest is the question of job displacement. In Chapter 1, I cautioned against misinterpretation of "job-counting" studies involving trade in general. This warning must be doubly emphasized when applied to multinationals since multinational trade and trade conducted through other institutional arrangements can be substitutes for each other. The dangers in job counting have not stopped the arguments, which reached the level of polemics as the Trade Act of 1974 was being debated. Business groups tended to downplay displacement or to point to job "gains." Union spokesmen painted "horror stories" of plants being dismantled and shipped overseas.

The limitations of the job-counting approach as applied to multinationals is best illustrated by a study conducted by the Tariff Commission at the behest of the Senate Finance Committee. When an important congressional committee asks for an estimate of job displacement, the recipient government agency must come up with something. The Tariff Commission economists, however, as if to demonstrate the futility of job counting, produced a spectrum of estimates ranging from a net "loss" of jobs to a net "gain."[3]

Three assumptions were used to generate estimates for what was termed "Case 1" in the Tariff Commission report: (1) The multinational corporation's (MNC) foreign investment increases the capital stock of the host country. It does not substitute for an investment a foreigner would have made, and the foreigner would not have made it in the MNC's absence. (2) Domestic investment in the United States is not reduced by the MNC's foreign investment. (3) U.S. exports could have substituted completely for affiliates' production abroad.

Under these three assumptions, table 5.2 shows that a gross job "loss" of almost 2.4 million was calculated for 1970 (column (1)). Various offsets were then estimated. These were headquarters employment attributed to foreign operations, U.S. exports to MNC affiliates abroad, the stimulation of exports from the United States generated by MNC investment abroad, and employment in the United States of foreign-based MNCs. The offsets—columns (2)-(5) of table 5.2—were subtracted from the gross job "loss" to produce a net job "loss" of 1.3 million. This estimate was considered an extreme case by the Tariff Commission, although assumptions could have been made that would have increased the "loss" further. For example, it might have been assumed that U.S. domestic investment (and employment) would have fallen as a result of foreign investment by U.S. firms.

If we assume that some of the investment abroad by U.S.-based MNCs would have been made by foreigners if the U.S. firms had not made them, then the gross job "loss" attributed to MNCs must decline. Similarly, the offsetting "gain" of employment from U.S. operations of foreign-based MNCs must also decline. Since no estimate is available of the degree of substitutability of MNC operations—how much of the activity would have occurred under different auspices in the absence of MNCs—the Tariff Commission took an arbitrary 50 percent rate for Case 2. That is, 50 percent of the foreign operations of U.S.-based MNCs were assumed to be mere substitutes for what would have occurred anyway. And 50 percent of the U.S. employment of foreign-based MNCs was assumed to substitute for what would have been employment in U.S. domestic firms. These two assumptions brought down the net job "loss" to 418,000.

Case 2 essentially represents a relaxation of assumption "1." Case 3 shows the effect of relaxing assumption "3," while retaining assumption "1." The Tariff Commission attempted to

Table 5.2. Tariff Commission Estimates of MNC Employment Impact, 1970 (thousands of employees)

| | Gross job "loss" (1) | Offsets to gross "loss" | | | | Net job "loss" (6) |
		MNC headquarters employment attributed to foreign production (2)	Effect of MNC exports to affiliates abroad (3)	Income effect of direct investment abroad (4)	U.S. employment of foreign MNCs (5)	
Case 1	−2,379	140	287	34	621	−1,297
Case 2	−1,190	140	287	34	311	−418
Case 3	−603	140	287	34	630	+488

SOURCE: U.S. Senate, Committee on Finance, *Implications of Multinational Firms for World Trade and Investment and for U.S. Trade and Labor* (Washington, D.C.: U.S. Government Printing Office, 1973), pp. 652, 665, 670.

NOTE: See text for assumptions behind each case.

compute what proportion of the overseas activity of U.S.-based MNCs could have been replaced by supply (exports) from the United States. One way of determining what U.S. domestic industry might have been able to export would be to project exports on the basis of the American share of developed-country exports by industry from some base period. The commission chose 1960–61 as a base period because it felt these were years of "high performance" for U.S. industry in world trade. The impact of imposing the base period is to limit the degree to which U.S. exports could have stepped in to replace foreign affiliate production. Assumption "3" sets the degree of potential replacement at 100 percent. But the 1960–61 base period reduces the rate of potential displacement substantially. The gross job "loss" of 2.4 million under Case 1 is reduced to 603,000 in Case 3.

In order to achieve symmetry, the Tariff Commission assumed that if foreign shares of developed-country exports had been held to 1960–61 levels, foreign-based MNCs would have invested more in the U.S. because the foreign shares of developed-country exports in fact rose after 1960–61. If production abroad was hypothetically limited to 1960–61 shares, the commission reasoned that foreigners would have invested more in the United States to make up the gap between actual and projected production. The impact of this adjustment was to raise the U.S. employment of foreign-based MNCs by about 9,000 jobs, a relatively minor effect.

Case 3 succeeds in greatly lowering gross job "loss" and slightly increasing one of the offsets. As a result, it produces an estimate of a net job "gain" of 488,000. Thus the Tariff Commission study produces estimates of the job impact ranging from -1.3 million to +488,000. Other studies have produced similar ranges.[4] Any study likely will produce comparable ambiguity. The MNCs certainly have advantages in their institutional arrangements that permit them greater coordination and access to information. But the net result of this advantage cannot be determined. Moreover, as already stressed, the key to the level of unemployment is job mobility and aggregate demand policy. None of the recent job-counting studies produce measures of job mobility or potential structural problems. And there is no evidence that the presence of MNCs produces a systematically different federal aggregate demand policy.

Impact on Capital and Technology

Multinationals might hurt labor indirectly by exporting American capital that otherwise would be employed at home. This is really an income-related, rather than an employment-related, argument since there is not fixed and rigid relationship between the number of jobs and the amount of capital. But it is usually assumed that countries with higher capital-to-labor ratios will provide higher standards of living for their workers.[5]

Multinationals do engage in international movements of capital, and certain elements in U.S. tax laws create artificial incentives to invest and reinvest abroad, since the resulting earnings are not subject to American taxes until they are repatriated. The reaction to date has been to create similar incentives for keeping export production at home through the creation of domestic international sales corporations (DISCs). Many observers believe that the creation of a domestic tax loophole to counteract a foreign loophole was inappropriate. Much has been written about this question of fiscal policy, but from labor's point of view, a more fundamental issue must be raised.

The impact of multinationals on capital flows is extremely difficult to isolate because, as noted earlier, direct investment is at least partially a substitute for other types of lending/borrowing activity. But even if this hurdle could be overcome, it is important to recall that multinational activity most often involves financial transactions rather than actual movement of capital equipment. Of course, multinationals may buy capital equipment in the United States and export it abroad. Indeed, the production and overseas sale of such equipment is an important component of U.S. manufacturing exports. But usually when the capital movements of multinationals are discussed, what is meant is movements of funds, not movements of goods.

Financial capital and physical capital are very different. If a country is a net importer of financial capital, it may use the proceeds either to buy foreign capital goods directly or to produce them itself, using the proceeds to substitute imported consumption goods for home production of consumption goods. In some cases, the inflow of financial capital may not lead to any increase in real capital; it may wind up entirely as increased consumption. The key factor is that a financial capital flow from one country to another may or may not lead to less real capital in the lender and/or more real capital in the borrower.

Even more ambiguity is introduced in the specific case of the United States. Until 1971, the international monetary system was based on a fixed value of the American dollar. In effect, this committed foreign governments to support the dollar, that is, to lend to the United States when the American balance of payments was in deficit. The United States did in fact experience balance-of-payments problems during the 1960s. Thus the expansion of U.S. multinationals abroad may well have been financed by foreigners through the roundabout channel of the international monetary system up to 1971. [6]

Finally, the capital question must be put into perspective. In 1968, the total value of "reproducible" capital assets—plant, equipment, and inventories—was estimated at $2.4 trillion. U.S. direct investments abroad in that year were valued at $65 billion. Net direct investments (subtracting the value of foreign direct investments in the United States) were about $54 billion. The total net investment position of the United States—including gold, official reserves, and nondirect investments—was $66 billion. Thus if the United States had somehow liquidated its entire net foreign portfolio and used the proceeds for investment at home, the overall stock of reproducible capital would have risen less than 3 percent.

Technology sometimes is embodied in capital equipment. In principle, the United States could try to limit the outflow of technology by selectively banning exports of sophisticated machinery. This has been done on occasion, but for national defense rather than "economic" reasons. The long-run effect of such a policy can easily be self-defeating, since it encourages the production of such equipment abroad. Technology is not really a machine; it is an idea, and it is extremely difficult to prevent the flow of ideas.

Industrial Relations Practices of MNCs

The industrial relations policies of MNCs are quite varied, as are other management policies. Sometimes local management abroad is allowed almost complete autonomy in dealing with industrial relations problems. Sometimes headquarters exerts a considerable influence. As might be expected, purely local matters such as employee grievances are pretty much left to local management discretion. Matters which could have corporationwide impact, such as strike settlement and collective bargaining, more often entail some headquarters involvement. In personnel matters with regard to management employees—where international mobility is possible—international corporate policy sometimes is required.

Wage policies of MNCs are closely related to local labor market conditions. This means that wages paid by MNCs generally are lower abroad than they are in the United States. International wage comparisons are difficult to make. Labor compensation abroad often is paid partially in the form of heavy payroll taxes to finance social insurance and welfare programs. Thus comparison must be made in terms of total compensation rather than the base wage rate. Moreover, wages vary across industries depending largely on the skill levels of the average worker required. So it is also necessary to provide some standardization for composition of industry.

Table 5.3 presents the result of a Tariff Commission attempt to compare hourly compensation paid in eight countries (including the United States) by U.S.-based MNCs with wages paid by all firms. The table shows the estimated hourly compensation expressed in dollars paid by the MNCs. Because of the sampling method, the data are approximate. A plus (+) sign following the estimated compensation means that the MNC average was greater than the all-firm average. A minus (-) sign indicates that the MNC compensation was somewhat less. No sign means that the MNC average and the all-firm average were identical. All figures are rounded to the nearest ten cents per hour.

The tendency for foreign wages to be less than U.S. wages is quite clear from table 5.3 U.S.-based MNCs seem to pay more on the average than their domestic counterparts in the U.S. They seem to pay somewhat less than domestic counterparts in Western Europe, but more in the two developing countries shown on the table (Brazil and Mexico). Some of these differences may reflect systematic differences in the skill mix or geographical location of the U.S.-based MNCs. The table does not permit a comparison on a detailed enough level to clarify the reasons for the difference.

Outside the U.S., the MNCs exhibited better productivity performance than their local counterparts. Thus their unit labor costs tended to be below the all-firm average. In the United States, however, the MNC productivity performance was about average, so that their unit labor costs were somewhat above the all-firm average. U.S.-based MNCs may have been at a labor-cost advantage relative to local competitors in 1970, and this disequilibrium situation accounts for some of their expansion. Profits of majority-owned foreign affiliates were above those of their U.S. parents in 1970. But this may reflect the recession in the United States that year.[7] Moreover, transfer pricing distorts such comparisons.

The foreign labor-cost advantage in 1970 relative to the United States had been eroding. Foreign wages rose faster than U.S. wages during the 1960s, as can be seen in table 5.4. This tendency was accelerated further by the dollar devaluation beginning in 1971. And, of course, the devaluation was part of the adjustment of the U.S. to previous overvaluation of the dollar which had tended to exaggerate the cost gap. But even in 1970—prior to the devaluation—labor costs were not the only element of costs affecting the location of international production.

Table 5.3.   Estimated Hourly Compensation of U.S. Multinational Firms, 1970*

Sector	U.S.	Canada	United Kingdom	Belgium-Luxemburg	France	West Germany	Brazil	Mexico
All Manufacturing	$5.50	$3.90	$1.70	$2.20	$2.40	$2.90	$1.00	$1.30
Food	4.10+	3.30+	1.80–	1.80–	1.70–	2.10–	.80+	1.00+
Paper	4.10–	4.40+	1.60–	2.00–	2.00–	2.40–	1.00+	1.20–
Chemicals	5.10+	4.00	1.70–	2.70–	2.70–	3.20–	.80–	1.60+
Rubber	4.60+	4.10+	1.80–	2.00–	2.20–	2.60–	1.10+	1.40+
Primary + fabricated metals	5.10+	4.00–	1.40–	2.50+	2.00–	2.60–	1.00+	1.10+
Nonelectrical machinery	5.70+	4.20	1.80–	2.40–	2.90–	3.40–	1.40+	1.50+
Electrical machinery	5.30+	3.70	1.60–	2.20–	2.60–	3.10	.70–	1.10+
Transportation equipment	5.50+	4.40	2.30–	2.60	2.50	3.40	1.20+	1.50+
Textiles + apparel	3.20+	2.60+	1.80–	1.70+	1.80–	2.10–	n.a.	1.10+
Lumber, wood, furniture	4.70+	2.80–	n.a.	n.a.	1.90–	2.30	n.a.	n.a.
Printing + publishing	n.a.	3.70–	n.a.	n.a.	n.a.	n.a.	n.a.	n.a.
Stone, clay, glass	4.90+	3.50–	1.40–	2.20	2.00–	3.20–	.90+	.80+
Instruments	5.80+	3.50–	1.70–	2.30–	3.00–	3.00+	n.a.	n.a.
Other manufacturing	4.00+	3.20	1.70–	1.60–	1.50–	2.40–	n.a.	.80–

SOURCE: U.S. Senate, Committee on Finance, *Implications of Multinational Firms for World Trade and Investment and for U.S. Trade and Labor* (Washington, D.C.: U.S. Government Printing Office, 1973), pp. 732–33.

*Figures rounded to nearest 10¢. See text for definition of plus and minus signs.

There is no way of knowing the degree to which labor costs explain the overall development of MNCs. Again, this is because even where labor costs are paramount, other institutions might

Table 5.4.   Average Annual Percent Change in Manufacturing
Hourly Compensation, 1960–1973, in U.S. dollars

Country	Annual change
U.S.	5.2
Canada	6.4
Japan	12.7
Belgium	8.6
Denmark	10.8
France	9.0
West Germany	6.4
Italy	12.2
Netherlands	10.3
Sweden	9.1
Switzerland	6.3
United Kingdom	9.9

SOURCE: *Monthly Labor Review*, November 1973, pp. 15–18, July 1975, p. 31.

have taken advantage of wage differences between countries, had MNCs not done so. As already noted, in the shoe and textile industries where labor costs are very important, most imports are not internal transactions of MNCs. Given limited available data, it is not possible to say whether foreign operations were more profitable than domestic in recent years, that is, whether a large disequilibrium existed.

American unions have been interested domestically in "taking wages out of competition." This phrase does not have a precise meaning, but it connotes coordinating wages between firms or plants in an industry so that competition on the basis of labor costs is lessened or controlled. Thus there has been considerable interest in the possibility of coordinated international collective bargaining with MNCs.

One of the difficulties that is always noted when the possibility of international collective bargaining is discussed is the differences between industrial relations systems between countries.[8] The only country with a system close to the U.S. model is Canada, where a heavy majority of union members—especially in the private sector—are affiliated with U.S.-based unions. The role of unions is perceived to be about the same in Canada as it is in the U.S.—to improve conditions through bargaining. (Quebec is something of a exception, since industrial relations in that province take on a European flavor.) Many of the larger firms in Canada are in fact subsidiaries of U.S.-based corporations. Hence, the perception of management regarding the role of unions in the two countries is similar. For these reasons, it is not surprising that the only examples of true coordinated collective bargaining take place along the U.S.-Canada border.[9]

Even in the U.S.-Canada context, the scope of such bargaining is limited. The primary example is the automobile industry, where the same union and the same firms operate in both countries. Even in this case, the notion of "wage parity" between the United States and Canadian automobile industries did not become a major union demand until the industry was integrated through the special free trade agreement on new cars. After "parity" was achieved, Canadian workers still earned less than U.S. workers because the concept was defined in terms of nominal dollars—Canadian and American. Only when the U.S. dollar and the Canadian dollar began to exchange at close to a one-for-one ratio was true parity achieved.

Outside the United States and Canada, the concept of an exclusive bargaining agent is not widespread. In Britain, for example, where institutions might be similar to those in the United States, a number of unions operate in what would be a single bargaining unit in American practice. Attempts to impose Taft-Hartley-type regulation of industrial relations have not proved successful. In France, not all unions would agree with the premise that their role is primarily collective bargaining. The largest union federation is the communist-led Confederation Génèrale du Travail (CGT). In the early postwar period, the CGT did not even accept the idea of dealing with capitalist enterprises. As might be expected, agreements of fixed duration are rare in France, and the various competing union federations often do not coordinate among themselves, let alone with unions in other countries.

Legal systems vary from country to country. In Australia, industrial relations are heavily influenced by an elaborate system of compulsory arbitration. Settlements follow a national pattern set by a court system, but are also affected by a layer of de facto bargaining in some industries. In fascist Spain, there are no independent unions apart from the state-endorsed organization. Some less-developed countries are characterized by "political" unions linked to the government. Finally, the American system of labor law is not especially supportive of international bargaining. An American union that struck on behalf of a foreign ally might be committing an unfair labor practice.

Such fringe benefits as pensions, holidays, and vacations that are left largely to private determination in the United States are established by law rather than by a negotiated agreement abroad. Grievance handling, which is generally established by collective bargaining in the United States, sometimes is left to official labor courts in other countries.

Even wage determination more often involves government policy abroad than it does in the American system. European countries have shown a greater willingness to experiment with "incomes policies" (wage/price controls) than has been seen— until recently—in the United States. In less-developed countries, minimum wage setting has a greater impact on the general level of wages than it does in the United States, since more workers are paid at or close to the legal minimum.

As in the case of other labor aspects of international trade, multinational bargaining need not be considered solely in the context of multinational firms. In the domestic economy, unions have found it advantageous to coordinate wage policy between firms under separate ownership which compete in the same product market. The relative wages paid by competing firms helps to determine the distribution of employment between the firms. Firms with a wage-cost advantage and no offsetting disadvantages can underbid competitors and capture their business. Conflict is inherent in establishing interfirm wage policy, although unions may not perceive it explicitly. Workers in firms that traditionally have been low payers would naturally like to have their wages raised to parity with other firms, but they would not like to see a decline in employment opportunities as a result. These conflicts are not insurmountable in the domestic economy. The internal political apparatus of the union may be able to achieve an acceptable compromise.

Since domestic firms in other countries also may be competitors in the American product market, multinational bargaining may appear advantageous to U.S. unions even if no multinationals are involved. The multinational, however, could stimulate the development of multinational bargaining. The fact that the different unions are dealing with the same employer may further the perception of unity of interests. Moreover, it may be helpful to have a single organization to meet with, rather than a collection of single employers. At the present, of course, unions in different countries often have a hard time pinning down the locus of decision making in MNCs. If real bargaining muscle developed on the labor side, a central negotiating body would have to be formed within the MNC.

Labor spokesmen sometimes argue that the development of the MNC adds a new dimension in bargaining. Multinational firms can utilize their far-flung resources to neutralize union pressure. For example, during a strike, an MNC might be able to reallocate production from the struck facility to a plant in another country. Of course, even without MNCs, a strike may lead customers to purchase imports and hence temporarily raise production abroad. But a domestic firm that is struck loses its customers—at least for a time—while the MNC can continue its normal relations with buyers. Representatives of MNCs argue that it is not easy to reallocate production and that the issue has been exaggerated.

Attempts have been made to establish multinational bargaining, some of them under the auspices of the International Trade Secretariats. The secretariats are international organizations composed of national unions in a common industry or group of industries. One of the most active in establishing coordinated bargaining has been the International Metalworkers' Federation, which, largely because of the membership of the United Automobile Workers, became interested in the subject in the 1950s. More recently, it has established subcommittees for each of the major multinational automobile firms. Unions dealing with these firms can meet and exchange information.

The International Federation of Chemical and General Workers' Unions has claimed great successes in dealing with MNCs and in preventing them from reallocating production during strikes. However, recent disclosures suggest that much of the activity was largely a matter of adroit public relations, rather than any substantive move toward coordinated bargaining.[10] There has been a tendency by advocates of multinational bargaining in this area to declare an occasional informal meeting of an MNC with representatives of a trade secretariat to be a great success for their approach.

At the present time, therefore, the only true multinational bargaining is occurring between the United States and Canada. Future breakthroughs are likely to take place within the newly enlarged European Common Market, where there are already some international union institutions. If inter-European bargaining becomes coordinated, there may be a greater possibility of U.S.-European bargaining. Cooperation between American unions and unions in less-developed countries, in the sense of true joint negotiations, is the least likely. Unions in less-developed countries probably would be most suspicious of the motives behind offers of cooperation from U.S. unions. They would not want to bargain themselves out of employment opportunities.

On the other hand, contacts between U.S. unions and unions in other countries have a long history and certainly will continue. The AFL-CIO has engaged in educational and other programs designed to assist and promote friendly relations with unions in other nations. Such contacts may open the way for coordinated multinational bargaining in the future, but they should not be confused with it at present. U.S. unions with problems of import competition must recognize that they will not find short-term relief from coordinated negotiations.

A related area is that of "international fair labor standards."

The International Labor Organization (ILO) was founded with the purpose of encouraging member countries to adopt uniform minimum standards of protective labor legislation. Part of the rationale for international standards was to avoid competition based on the costs of maintaining such standards between countries. The idea of labor-cost uniformity has been traced as far back as the late eighteenth century.[11]

Only one effort has been made to incorporate international fair labor standards into an international treaty. The General Agreement on Tariffs and Trade (GATT) originally was concluded as a prelude to the creation of an international trade organization. Article 7 of the charter of this proposed organization called for "maintenance of fair labour standards related to productivity." But the organization never came into existence, and the current GATT does not contain reference to international fair labor standards.

Union groups, both domestic and international, periodically have called for adherence to international fair labor standards. Precise definitions of the term are rarely offered. Sometimes it seems to involve comparisons of wages between the exporting industry or firm and the general level of wages in the exporting country. Exactly how interregional or interoccupational wage differentials would be treated under such a definition is unclear. At one point, the AFL-CIO suggested that comparisons of unit labor costs would be appropriate.[12] Sometimes the phrase is taken to cover industrial relations practices such as the recognition of independent trade unions. For example, there have been complaints that some foreign-based MNCs operating in the United States have adopted an antiunion stance.

Proponents of international fair labor standards do not mean to apply them exclusively to multinational corporations. Even if such standards were required through international agreement, it is doubtful that U.S. import-competing industries would obtain much relief. Foreign governments would be unlikely to agree to standards that severely affected their ability to export. Even the ILO seems to have begun to question the economic effects of some of its standards on employment opportunities in less-developed countries.

The Special Case of Items 806.30 and 807.00

Two items in the Tariff Schedules of the United States have been the subject of recent controversy.[13] Item 806.30 originated in the Customs Simplification Act of 1956. Its sponsor in the House of Representatives wished to obtain special tariff treatment for metal articles partially processed in Canada during plant breakdowns in the United States. A duty exemption is permitted for the American content of a product exported for processing and then returned for further processing in the U.S. That is, duty is paid only on the value added abroad which presumably would have a high labor content. The Senate Finance Committee took a broader view of the intent of item 806.30 and did not limit its application to imports from Canada to the United States.

Item 807.00 first entered the Tariff Schedules in 1963, but it incorporated established practice in customs assessment which originated in a court decision in 1954. The decision interpreted the Tariff Act of 1930 (Smoot-Hawley Tariff) to permit the re-importation without duty of U.S.-made components in foreign-assembled products. Until 1963, duty was not assessed on the component as long as it could be removed from the imported product without sustaining injury. Subsequent interpretations and legislative amendments substantially liberalized item 807.00. Under current procedures, it is only necessary to show that the components were in fact American-made and that "they have not lost their physical identity . . . and have not been advanced in value or improved . . . except by the assembly abroad."[14] Imports under 806.30 and 807.00 amounted to 6.2 percent of total imports for consumption in 1973, up from 3.7 percent in 1966. Item 807.00 accounted for almost 50 percent of imports under the two provisions.

The arguments surrounding these items of the Tariff Schedules are by now familiar to the reader. Obviously, the items permit labor-intensive assembly services to be imported, which could not be imported profitably if the entire product was subject to tariff. To the extent that U.S. production is displaced, unemployment in the United States might result *if* there are significant structural/mobility problems in the affected industries. In the longer run, a shift to less labor-intensive production in the United States might have a negative effect on real wages. [15] But unemployment in the absence of a structural/mobility problem is largely a function of federal aggregate demand policy, not imports. And the possibility of a real wage impact stems from an abstract theory whose actual application is uncertain.

Because of special attention received by imports from American plants in Mexico, it might be assumed that foreign assembly operations are largely taking place in affiliates of U.S.-based MNCs. However, according to a 1969 survey by the Tariff Commission, only 40 percent of item 807.00 imports and 58 percent of item 806.30 imports fell into this category. [16] The rest of the imports came from foreign firms that incorporate U.S. components into their products and export their output to the United States through arms-length contracts with domestic U.S. firms. As has been pointed out previously, problems associated with MNCs also can arise under other institutional arrangements.

It is not evident that items 806.30 or 807.00 would cause net displacement of production in the United States. If the two items were eliminated, any one of three changes might be made in production patterns. In some cases, it might be profitable to discontinue foreign assembly and perform all operations in the United States or to continue foreign assembly even with the duty required on the full product. (This would be the case if the duty on the entire product were sufficiently low so that foreign assembly still would be cheaper than U.S. processing.) Finally, it might turn out that the *entire* product—including what are presently U.S.-made components—would be manufactured abroad.

The third possibility can be illustrated with a simple example. Suppose that U.S.-made components cost $7.00 and U.S. assembly labor costs $4.00 per unit of output. Unit costs for complete production in the U.S. are therefore $11.00. Suppose foreign unit costs are $6.00 for components and $3.00 for assembly labor and that there is a 20 percent American duty on imports of the product. The imported unit cost is $9.00 plus the 20 percent tariff, or $10.80. Thus, without special tariff treatment, a firm would choose to import the entire product rather than produce any of it in the United States. If, however, U.S. components can be exported and returned after assembly duty-free, with a 20 percent tariff paid only on foreign value added, there will be partial production in the United States. Component production costs per unit of final product would be $7.00. Foreign assembly costs would be $3.00 plus 20 percent, or $3.60. Hence, a combination of U.S. component production, foreign assembly, and a tariff only on foreign value added would lead to imported unit costs of $10.60. Since $10.60 is the cheapest alternative, the impact of special tariff treatment is to preserve some production in the U.S. Under the 20 percent tariff with no special treatment, all production—including component manufacturing—would take place abroad.

A survey by the Tariff Commission in 1969 of importers under items 806.30 and 807.00 suggested that if the items were eliminated, the tendency would be to transfer *all* production abroad. The commission estimated that about thirty-seven thousand American jobs were involved in the processing of components for foreign assembly, and presumably most of these would be "displaced" by a repeal of the items. [17] However, the AFL-CIO did not accept the commission's views and has continued to oppose the special tariff provisions.

As noted in Chapter 2, from an economic viewpoint trade and immigration are somewhat interchangeable. Obviously, different social consequences result from the importation of immigrants, as opposed to the importation of labor embodied in goods. But it might be expected that if emigration possibilities are restricted from a labor-abundant country, market forces will tend to push that country into the production of labor-intensive exports. Such activities need not involve multinational operations; however, in the case of the Mexican Border Development Program, a considerable amount of multinational activity is involved.

Mexico is clearly a labor-abundant country compared to the United States. For many years, legally and illegally, Mexican laborers flowed across the border into the United States. Mexico fostered capital-intensive production in its internal manufacturing sector through a restrictive quota system that shielded local enterprises from foreign competition. International economic theory suggests that such a policy would tend to depress the demand for labor and real wages, although the same qualifications which were made when applying that theory to the United States must be made in this case as well. A recent International Labor Organization study suggests that the combination of internal import substitution and a minimum wage floor created a substantial problem of underutilization of labor in Mexico. [18]

In recent years, the Mexican government has attempted to foster labor-intensive exports to the United States, taking advantage of items 806.30 and 807.00. This policy shift can be attributed in part to the reduction in legal opportunities for migration to the United States, especially the ending of the "bracero" program for agricultural labor. In effect, as international economic theory suggests, if workers are unable to come to the factories, the factories may be brought to the workers.

Under the border program, firms are permitted to establish facilities within twelve and a half miles of the frontier. These facilities are allowed to import components for assembly without duty exclusively for export back to the United States. A "twin-plant" concept is emphasized so that components are ferried between the Mexican plant and its U.S. counterpart. The firms taking advantage of this program do not have to be American-owned. In fact, multinational Japanese firms have moved in and substituted twin operations for Asian production, a development reinforcing the Tariff Commission report. Most of the firms, however, are U.S.-based and produce such items as apparel, electronics, and toys. Their Mexican employment was estimated at forty thousand workers in 1972, many of them teenage girls or young women. [19] Mexican exports through item 807.00 have risen rapidly, from 0.8 percent of item 807.00 imported in 1966, to 8.8 percent in 1969, and 15.6 percent in 1973.

There is no doubt that the Border Development Program poses a dilemma for the United States and that the Tariff Commission may be right in its conclusions. U.S. jobs in the industries most affected would be displaced if items 806.30 and 807.00 were removed, though the allocation of the effects may be uneven. The types of jobs "preserved" by items 806.30 and 807.00 may be relatively skilled compared to those employed in foreign assembly. The regional impact on the United States may vary. Presumably, even if the Tariff Commission is correct in the aggregate, a repeal of 806.30 and 807.00 might not totally eliminate adversely affected U.S. industries. Some local production might continue, even if at a reduced scale. Even if the overall impact of 806.30 and 807.00 is to preserve production in the United States, near the border region U.S. employment and/or income opportunites for unskilled low-wage jobs are adversely affected.

But even this limited conclusion might be qualified. The Mexican Border Development Program was partially a reaction to increased U.S. immigration restrictions. There may be a trade-off between imports from the border area and illegal immigration. Some observers have become quite concerned about the social impact on the United States of a class of illegal alien workers. Choking the import channel could intensify this problem.

In many respects, the issues involved with multinational operations under 806.30 and 807.00 are no different from other issues raised by economic relations in an inequitable world. Living standards across countries vary widely. In many parts of the world, industrial conditions approximate those which existed in the United States in the year 1900 or even before. This fact of life creates pressure for immigration to high-wage areas and/or labor-intensive exports. There are costs and benefits of either of these channels to the recipient country, and these costs and benefits need not spread themselves out in an equitable fashion. The issues posed by international commerce serve to remind the United States of the moral and social dilemmas which plague the modern world and our domestic economy.

The Government-Business Nexus Abroad

As noted earlier, host government attitudes toward foreign multinational firms are ambiguous. At times, host governments will attempt to attract foreign investment through special tax treatment or subsidies. American tariff law requires that any foreign bounties paid to stimulate exports to the United States must be offset by the imposition of a countervailing tariff as determined by the U.S. Customs Service. The countervailing tariff must be imposed; no finding that a domestic industry is being injured is required.

Of course, in many cases foreign subsidies are hidden. They may apply, for example, to inputs used by the firm, rather than directly to its output. Often, however, what appear to be subsidies or preferential treatment may simply represent an attempt to compensate for artificially imposed disadvantages. For example, in the Mexican case described above, border firms are allowed to bring materials into Mexico without being subject to Mexican tariffs or quotas. This is in recognition of the fact that such tariffs and quotas make production costs artificially high in Mexico and tend to limit exports.

Proponents of protection often point to foreign barriers to U.S. exports and foreign incentives to export to the United States as proof that the United States faces "unfair" competition. Actually, just as the welfare effects of tariffs and other distortions in the United States are hard to quantify, so are the effects of similar measures abroad. It is not clear that countries that engage heavily in such practices are doing themselves a favor, although they clearly are doing a favor to their domestic industrial interests that are directly involved. Probably one of the biggest barriers to U.S. exports is *American* barriers to imports. Import barriers raise the internal costs of inputs to production relative to world prices, thus putting U.S. exporters at a disadvantage (as in the Mexican case). More indirectly, barriers to imports reduce the flow of dollars into world currency markets and tend to raise the price of the dollar (the exchange rate) relative to what it otherwise would be. This exchange-rate effect also raises U.S. production costs relative to the world and limits export opportunities.

In some cases, foreign firms appear to subsidize their own exports to the United States, a practice known as "dumping." The phrase "dumping" is obviously meant to be pejorative, but to the economist it is simply a form of price discrimination. A product is said to be dumped in the United States if it is sold to American buyers at lower prices than apply to the firm's customers in its home market. Under U.S. tariff law, action is taken against dumping only if a domestic industry can be shown to be injured. The investigation begins at the Customs Service. If dumping is found to be occurring, the International Trade Commission seeks evidence of domestic injury. In cases of injury, countervailing duties are assessed. The foreign supplier can escape the charge of dumping by lowering its home price, a practice unlikely to have any beneficial effect on U.S. domestic competitors.

Dumping is superficially similar to export subsidies, but the cause is likely to be different. Subsidies result from explicit government action. Dumping often reflects a lesser degree of competition in the home market than in the United States, which may reflect the home government's policy. For example, foreign antitrust laws—if they exist—may not be strictly enforced. Or it may reflect a predatory attempt to eliminate U.S. competition in industries with high re-entry costs. Finally, dumping may result from a temporary spell of overproduction by an oligopolistic firm which does not want to start a price war at home by "spoiling" its domestic market.

Whatever the cause for a lower price for exports—dumping or subsidy—the impact on U.S. labor is determined mainly by the characteristics of the import-competing industry. A large degree of immobility may lead to actual unemployment or under-employment. It is unlikely, however, that foreign subsidies or dumping have much overall impact. Subsidies are frowned on by international treaties such as the General Agreement on Tariffs and Trade (GATT). Persistent dumping probably reflects a foreign cost advantage—as in the case of inexpensive Japanese-made TV sets which were dumped in the U.S. market. Even if the dumping margin is eliminated, the foreign source still is likely to be a potent competitor.

The political balance in most countries seems usually to result in some form of internal protection. As noted earlier, limits on imports translate eventually into limits on exports. The overall impact of government distortions—at home and abroad—is to limit trade in all directions, exports and imports. Unless the magnitudes of individual distortions are suddenly changed, short-run labor displacements are unlikely to result. Longer-run implications are harder to predict, but the analysis would generally follow the lines given in Chapter 1. As with other issues sometimes associated with multinational firms, the impacts discussed need not be exclusively linked to multinationals. Similar effects can occur through arms-length transactions between purely domestic firms.

Conclusions

The treatment of multinational firms in this chapter will leave many readers unsatisfied. Because of the need to confine the analysis to the labor impact, many of the most interesting aspects of MNCs have been neglected. These aspects revolve around issues of national sovereignty, political influence, the impact on foreign policy, and the general area of the "goodness" or "badness" of bigness in business enterprises. Economics generally has little to say about such issues in the domestic setting, so perhaps it is not surprising that the problem of a lack of a framework for analysis is compounded in the case of multinational firms.

It is important, however, to stress that multinational firms are basically institutional arrangements for making transfers of goods, financial capital, technology, and management skills. Because each of these items can be transferred without the use of MNCs, their independent effect is hard to pin down, particularly in the manufacturing sector, which has attracted the greatest attention in terms of labor impact. But if MNCs are viewed as especially efficient transfer agents, it simply means that the fundamental factors which induce such transfers have come to have a greater impact. In international trade, these fundamental factors primarily involve relative costs of production between countries. These costs include, but are not confined to, labor costs.

Epilogue

There is no way of proving definitely whether international trade is good or bad for labor. Obviously, the effects are varied, some in opposing directions. The only current program specifically aimed at a trade-related labor injury is that of providing adjustment assistance to displaced workers. Even in that program, which is not aimed at long-run questions of income distribution, there are conceptual problems of separating trade impacts from other factors contributing to layoffs.

At the time the Trade Act of 1974 was under consideration, the rhetoric surrounding the trade-labor issue reached new peaks of shrillness. Proponents and opponents presented arguments with a level of fervor and certainty unwarranted by any empirical evidence actually produced. The worker adjustment assistance program under the old Trade Expansion Act of 1962 clearly was of limited help to trade-impacted workers. The program was liberalized, and during 1975 it has been "paying off" with regularity. But the policy problems inherent in a manpower program which defines eligibility by cause rather than effect remain unresolved.

There is reason to hope for a cooler climate to consider trade and labor issues in the near future. Because the Trade Act of 1974 has been passed, major trade legislation is unlikely to receive serious consideration for several years, during which time some reassessment is possible. The Trade Act required the establishment of a Labor Department data system to explore trade-related issues. Perhaps the studies that will be based on this data will go beyond the misleading "job-counting" efforts of the past and will tackle mobility and structural unemployment problems.

If nothing else, debate on the impact of trade on labor has highlighted an important aspect of all major economic problems. Debate over trade tends naturally to fall into an "us versus them" framework. In true mercantilist spirit, it is often assumed that there is but one national interest to be served, at the expense of "them"—the foreigner. In fact, "us" is composed of many groups with differing self-interests. Any broad policy will help some of us and hurt others in our midst. The ultimate resolution of such questions is left to the political process, and the best that can be hoped for is that the debate will be carried out in the context of reasonable estimates of where the benefits and losses lie.

Notes

Preface

1. Malcolm D. Bale, *"Adjustment to Freer Trade: An Analysis of the Adjustment Assistance Provisions of the Trade Expansion Act of 1962"* (Ph.D. diss., University of Wisconsin-Madison, 1973); James E. McCarthy, *"Trade Adjustment Assistance: A Case Study of the Shoe Industry in Massachusetts"* (Ph.D. diss., Tufts University, 1974). Both studies are discussed in Chapter 3, and both are available from the National Technical Information Service. A study by Charles R. Frank, Jr., is being sponsored by the Brookings Institution.

Chapter 1

1. U.S. Bureau of the Census, *U.S. Commodity Exports and Imports as Related to Output, 1970 and 1969* (Washington, D.C.: U.S. Government Printing Office, 1973), Table 1A.

2. Quoted from Economic Policy Committee to the AFL–CIO Executive Council, "International Trade," mimeographed, (February 1970), p. 2. This report was kindly supplied by Elizabeth Jager of the AFL–CIO Research Department.

3. Charles P. Kindleberger, *International Economics*, 5th ed. (Homewood, Ill.: Richard D. Irwin, 1973), p. 202.

4. David Ricardo, *The Principles of Political Economy and Taxation* (New York: E.P. Dutton, 1962), pp. 77–93.

5. This was first noted in the literature in 1941. See Wolfgang F. Stolper and Paul A. Samuelson, "Protection and Real Wages," in American Economic Association, *Readings in the Theory of International Trade* (Homewood, Ill.: Richard D. Irwin, 1950). pp. 333–57.

6. Wassily Leontief, "Domestic Production and Foreign Trade; The American Capital Position Re-examined," in Richard E. Caves and Harry G. Johnson, eds., *Readings in International Economics* (Homewood, Ill.: Richard D. Irwin, 1968), pp. 503–27.

7. Nontariff barriers such as quotas can have a significant economic impact. One author estimated that about three-fourths of the cost of U.S. trade restrictions were associated with such barriers. See Stephen P. Magee, "The Welfare Effects of Restrictions on U.S. Trade," *Brookings Papers on Economic Activity*, No. 3 (1972), pp. 645–01. Foreign nations may agree to "voluntary" quotas for two reasons. First, they may fear more severe restrictions will be imposed unless they cooperate. Second, in some cases the foreigner might actually gain. This could occur if the quota substantially raises the U.S. domestic price about to world levels. With a quota, foreigners may sell less in terms of volume, but they may make greater profits because of the differential.

8. The quote is from a statement by Nathaniel Goldfinger on behalf of the AFL–CIO in U.S., Congress, House, Committee on Foreign Affairs, *Trade Adjustment in Assistance*, 92d Cong., 2d sess., 1972, pp. 52–53.

9. Jerome A. Mark, "Progress in Measuring Productivity in Government," *Monthly Labor Review*, 95 (December 1972): 3–6.

10. The remarkable clothespins episode is described in Peter B. Kenan, *Giant Among Nations* (Chicago: Rand McNally, 1963), pp. 558–65.

11. Such an allegation can be found in Ingo Walter, "How a Trade Policy is Made: A Politico-Economic Decision System," in Robert G. Hawkins and Ingo Walters, eds., *The United States and International Markets* (Lexington, Mass.: Lexington Books, 1972), pp. 27–28. For a denial of this proposition by the AFL–CIO, see the testimony of Nathaniel Goldfinger in U.S., Congress, House, Committee on Foreign Affairs, *Trade Adjustment Assistance*, pp. 52–53.

12. Daniel J. B. Mitchell, "Labor and the Tariff Question," *Industrial Relations* 9 (May 1970): 268–76.

13. Some examples of the job-counting literature opposed to trade restrictions are Lawrence B. Krause, "How Much of Current Unemployment Did We Import?" *Brookings Papers on Economic Activity*, No. 2 (1971), pp. 417–27; United Nations Conference on Trade and Development, *Problems and Policies of Trade: Manufactures and Semi-Manufactures* III (New York: United Nations, 1968): 157–64; United Nations Conference on Trade and Development, *Adjustment Assistance Measures* (New York: United Nations, 1972), pp. 8–16. Eugene L. Stewart, "Import Competition and Governmental Relief," in Commission on International Trade and Investment Policy, *United States International Economic Policy in an Interdependent World* (Washington, D.C.: U.S. Government Printing Office, 1971), Papers I, pp. 193–288, especially p. 199, is an example of a job-counting paper favoring restriction. The same set of numbers can be subject to different interpretations. For example, in a special report, the Bureau of Labor Statistics estimated that jobs "attributed to" merchandise exports rose from 2.5 million in 1966 to 2.7 million in 1969. Job "displacement" by imports rose from 1.8 million to 2.5 million over the same period. Someone favoring trade liberalization could argue that in both years, the trade sector was a net positive provider of jobs, since the export jobs exceeded the import jobs. Someone arguing for trade restrictions could argue that the net positive job contribution of the trade sector had fallen from .7 million to .2 million during 1966–69, and therefore .5 million jobs had been "lost" because of international trade. See U.S. Bureau of Labor Statistics, "Foreign Trade and Employment," in Commission on International Trade and Investment Policy, *International Economic Policy*, Papers I, pp. 497–506.

14. U.S. Bureau of Labor Statistics, "Job Tenure of American Workers, January 1973" (Special Labor Force Report, May 1974), p. 6.

Chapter 2

1. Details of the calculations are not presented in this chapter. Information on sources and methodology may be found in Daniel J. B. Mitchell, "Recent Changes in the Labor Content of U.S. International Trade," *Industrial and Labor Relations Review* 28 (April 1975): 355–75. Input/output analysis was not used in the calculations. There has been some theoretical literature on whether input/output analysis is appropriate for this type of study; probably, it would have been appropriate although it would have increased the computational complexity and cost. However, as an empirical matter, it would have been unlikely to change the basic conclusions. For more on this point, see Donald B. Keesing, "Labor Skills and International Trade," *Review of Economics and Statistics* 47 (August 1965): 288; and Robert E. Baldwin, "Determinants of the Commodity Structure of U.S. Trade," *American Economic Review* 61 (March 1971), 132–33.

2. Four-firm concentration ratios at the four-digit standard industrial classification level were taken from the 1967 *Census of Manufactures.* These were averaged to the three-digit level. If the results were less than 25 percent, the industry was given a value of 1. Similarly, for 25 to 49 percent, the industry was given a 2; 50 to 74 percent a 3; 75 to 100 percent a 4. The industry indexes were weighted by exports or imports to produce the results shown on table 2.2. Concentration generally fell in the 25 to 49 percent range, a finding in line with Baldwin, "Determinants," p. 134, for 1962. The index was deliberately made relatively insensitive to minor changes since the connection between "competitiveness" and concentration ratio is imprecise. Only large changes in the index based on the 1965 and 1970 trade patterns would be worthy of attention.

3. When 1970 figures on shipments, depreciation, and full-time equivalent employees are used as a base for calculation, the depreciation-to-full-time equivalent employees ratios for overall trade in U.S. exports and imports were $1,686 and $1,502, respectively. For manufacturing, the corresponding figures are $1,309 and $1,171. When 1970 is used as a base to estimate the ratios of 1965, in both overall trade and manufacturing, imports appear slightly more labor-intensive than exports, even at the earlier date. However, the best method of calculation is to use the 1965 base figures to estimate the ratios for 1965 and the 1970 base figures to estimate the 1970 ratios. This procedure puts the reversal of relative labor-intensity somewhere between 1965 and 1970. It should be noted that no attempt was made to deflate depreciation by sector, in order to make the 1965-based and 1970-based figures more comparable.

4. It would not be correct to say that trade with Japan caused the reversal. Such a statement would be equivalent to saying that if Japan did not exist, U.S. exports would be relatively labor-intensive. However, if Japan did not exist, U.S. trade patterns with other countries would be different, and the resulting relative labor-intensity of exports to imports could not be determined from the data discussed in the text.

5. See Walter Fogel, "Mexican Labor in United States Labor Markets," and Michael J. Piore, "The 'New Immigration' and the Presumptions of Social Policy," in Industrial Relations Research Association, *Proceedings* (December 1974), pp. 343–49.

6. Thus, paradoxically, the presence of illegal aliens may preserve jobs and incomes of *some* members of the legal work force. That is, legals and illegals may be complementary in some cases.

Chapter 3

1. Commission on Foreign Economic Policy, *Report to the President and the Congress* (Washington, D.C.: U.S. Government Printing Office, 1954), pp. 54–58.

2. Cited in U.S., Congress, Senate, Committee on Finance, *Trade Expansion Act of 1962*, 87th Cong., 2nd sess., 1962, p. 246.

3. Citations of the various union positions can be found in Daniel J. B. Mitchell, *Essays on Labor and International Trade* (Los Angeles: Institute of Industrial Relations, UCLA, 1970), pp. 57–58.

4. The National Association of Manufacturers' (NAM) position can be found in U.S., Congress, Senate, Committee on Finance, *Trade Expansion Act of 1962*, pp. 1630–1631.

5. The Automobile Workers called—without success—for reinstatement of the adjustment assistance provisions of the APTA after they expired. See the statement of Douglas A. Fraser in U.S., Congress, House, Subcommittee on Foreign Economic Policy of the Committee on Foreign Affairs, *Trade Adjustment Assistance, Hearings*, 92nd Cong., 2nd sess., 1972, p. 340.

6. Under the original proposal, a few workers might have received higher benefits than under the TEA, but most would have received lower benefits. The original proposal specified benefits equal to 50 percent of a worker's average weekly wage up to a limit of two-thirds of his *state's* average weekly wage. The TEA provided benefits equal to 65 percent of a worker's earnings up to 65 percent of the *national* average weekly wage. Thus, a high-paid worker in a high-wage state might have received more under the original TA than under the TEA. See Charles R. Frank, Jr., *Adjustment Assistance: American Jobs and Trade with the Developing Countries* (Washington, D.C.; Overseas Development Council, 1973), pp. 36–40. It was inevitable that the Nixon administration benefit proposals would be modified. A consensus had already formed in Congress that benefits under the old TEA were inadequate. See U.S., Congress, House, Subcommittee on Foreign Economic Policy of the Committee on Foreign Affairs, *Trade Adjustment Assistance, Report*, 92nd Cong., 2nd sess., 1972, pp. 18–19.

7. Special Representative for Trade Negotiations, *Future United States Foreign Trade Policy* (Washington, D.C.: U.S. Government Printing Office, 1969), pp. 41–54.

8. Commission on International Trade and Investment Policy, *United States International Economic Policy in an Interdependent World* (Washington, D.C.: U.S. Government Printing Office, 1971), Report, pp. 45–59.

9. An NAM report entitled "Trade Adjustment Assistance" is reprinted in U.S., Congress, House, Committee on Ways and Means, *Trade Reform*, 93rd Cong., 1st sess., 1973, pp. 1929–2000.

10. The Chamber's position can be found in *ibid.*, p. 1383.

11. In his written statement before the House Ways and Mean Committee, Leonard Woodcock, president of the United Automobile Workers, points out that a majority of Chamber of Commerce members were willing to support a program more liberal than that proposed by the administration and more liberal than the provisions in the final TA. According to Woodcock, the Chamber set up a task force headed by C. Fred Bergsten of the Brookings Institution to study the issue. The task force's report was endorsed by a majority of the Chamber's

board of directors, but failed to gain the two-thirds vote required for adoption. See ibid., pp. 864–865.

12. For analyses of the provisions of the 1962 and 1965 laws, see Stanley D. Metzger, "Adjustment Assistance"; Marvin M. Fooks, "Trade Adjustment Assistance"; U.S. Bureau of Domestic Commerce, "Adjustment Assistance for U.S. Firms"; and U.S. Department of Labor, "Adjustment Assistance for Workers"; all in Commission on International Trade and Investment Policy, *Economic Policy,* Papers I, pp. 319–394. An analysis of the House-passed version of the TA adjustment assistance proposal can be found in U.S., Congress, Senate, Committee on Finance, *The Trade Reform Act of 1973,* 93d Cong., 2d sess., 1974, pp. 574–581.

13. A number of proposals would have required exporters, multinational corporations, or foreigners to pay for adjustment benefits. This may explain the eventual decision to use customs revenue. See U.S., Congress, Senate, Committee on Finance, *Trade Reform Act of 1973,* p. 177; U.S., Congress, Senate, Subcommittee on Foreign Economic Policy, *Hearings,* pp. 280, 332.

14. For a summary of this case, see "Shoe Workers Fail to Overturn U.S. Tariff Commission Ruling," *Daily Labor Report,* November 8, 1974, pp. A-3–A-5.

15. Stanley D. Metzger, "The Escape Clause and Adjustment Assistance: Proposals and Assessments," *Law and Policy in International Business* 2 (Summer 1970): 369.

16. See U.S. Tariff Commission, *Calculators, Typewriters, and Typewriter Parts:Workers of the Elmira, N.Y., Plant of Remington-Rand Division, Sperry Rand Corp.,* TC Publication 492 (Washington, D.C.: Tariff Commission, June 1972). See also Tracy W. Murray and Michael R. Edgmand, "Full Employment, Trade Expansion, and Adjustment Assistance," *Southern Economic Journal* 36 (April 1970), 418–19.

17. U.S. Tariff Commission, *Mercury-Wetted Contact Relays: Workers of the Rapid City, S. Dak., Plant of the C. P. Clare Co.,* TC publication 469 (Washington, D.C.: Tariff Commission, March 1972).

18. A review of adjustment assistance under the APTA can be found in Jeffrey A. Manley, "Adjustment Assistance: Experience under the Automotive Products Trade Act of 1965," *Harvard International Law Journal* 10 (Spring 1969): 294–315.

19. Metzger, "Escape Clause," p. 369.

20. U.S., Congress, Senate, Committee on Finance, *Canadian Automobile Agreement: Eighth Annual Report of the President to the Congress on the Operation of the Automotive Products Trade Act of 1965,* 94th Cong., 1st sess., 1974, p. 21; U.S., Congress, Senate, Committee on Finance, *Canadian Automobile Agreement: Third Annual Report of the President to Congress on the Operation of the Automotive Products Trade Act of 1965,* 91st Cong., 1st sess., 1969, pp. 12–13.

21. The TA income cap for a high-wage employee would be 130 percent of the manufacturing weekly wage. If the manufacturing wage were $185, the income cap on wages and TA benefits would be $240.50. For example, if such a worker earned $300 on a part-time basis after injury, he would be able to keep 50 percent of this amount and add it to his benefits were it not for the income cap. As a high-wage employee, his normal weekly benefit amount would be 100 percent of the manufacturing wage of $185. Thus, were it not for the income cap, he would be able to have a weekly income of $185 plus $150 or $335. However, the income cap would limit him to $240.50. Under TEA, his normal weekly benefit would

have been 65 percent of the manufacturing wage or $120.25. To this he would have added the full $150 for a total of $170.25. Thus, in theory, a case could arise in which a worker under TEA could collect more than under TA. In the case described above, the worker would have been better off in both instances to keep his $300 and not collect any adjustment payments. In general, peculiar examples of this type arise at higher wage levels that do not characterize trade-impacted workers, and at which it would not pay to collect benefits.

22. Malcolm D. Bale, "Adjustment to Freer Trade: An Analysis of the Adjustment Assistance Provisions of the Trade Expansion Act of 1962" (Ph.D. diss., University of Wisconsin-Madison, 1973), available from the National Technical Information Service.

23. James E. McCarthy, "Trade Adjustment Assistance: A Case Study of the Shoe Industry in Massachusetts" (Ph.D. diss., Tufts University, 1974), available from the National Technical Information Service.

24. See the statement of I. W. Abel on the part of the AFL–CIO in U.S. Congress, House, Committee on Ways and Means, *Trade Reform*, p. 1218.

25. This interpretation was given to the author by one official involved in the program.

Chapter 4

1. C. Fred Bergsten estimated that a somewhat more ambitious program would cost $500 million (not counting administration). See his testimony in U.S., Congress, House, Subcommittee on Foreign Economic Policy of the Committee on Foreign Affairs, *Trade Adjustment Assistance, Report*, 92d Cong., 2d sess., 1972, p. 132. Bergsten subsequently revised his estimate downward in response to criticism by Douglas Fraser of the Automobile Workers. See Fraser's comments and Bergsten's acknowledgement in the same volume, pp. 328–330, 409. The conference report on the TA estimated a benefit cost of $335 million. See U.S., Congress, Senate, Committee on Finance, *Trade Act of 1974: Summary of the Provisions of H. R. 10710*, 93d Cong., 2d sess., 1974, p. 8.

2. It must be emphasized that this figure is an upper-limit guess. If state unemployment insurance payments averaged 55 percent of the weekly wage, and if these benefits are extended to cover the full 52 weeks, unemployment insurance would be paying 55%/70% = 78.6% of the direct benefit costs.

3. For a review, see Stanley H. Ruttenberg, *Manpower Challenge of the 1970s: Institutions and Social Change* (Baltimore: Johns Hopkins Press, 1970); and Sar A. Levitan and Robert Taggart III, *Social Experimentation and Manpower Policy: The Rhetoric and the Reality* (Baltimore: Johns Hopkins Press, 1971).

4. See Charles C. Killingsworth, "Automation, Jobs, and Manpower: The Case for Structural Unemployment," in Garth L. Mangum, ed., *The Manpower Revolution: Its Policy Consequences* (Garden City, N.Y.: Doubleday, 1965), pp. 85–103.

5. See Charles C. Holt, C. Duncan MacRae, Stuart O. Schweitzer, and Ralph E. Smith, "Manpower Policies to Reduce Inflation and Unemployment," in Lloyd Ulman, ed., *Manpower Programs in the Policy Mix* (Baltimore: Johns Hopkins Press, 1973) pp. 51–82.

6. For a discussion of "Creaming," see Daniel S. Hammermesh, "The Secondary Effects of Manpower Programs," in Michael E. Borus, ed., *Evaluating the Impact of Manpower Programs* (Lexington, Mass.: Lexington Books, 1972), pp. 234–35.

7. Levitan and Taggart, *Social Experimentation*, pp. 49–51.

8. John P. Owen, John F. MacNaughton, and L. D. Belzung, *The Anatomy of a Workforce Reduction* (Houston: Center for Research in Business and Economics, College of Business Administration, University of Houston, 1966), p. 54.

9. Martin Schnitzer, *Regional Unemployment and the Relocation of Workers: The Experience of Western Europe, Canada, and the United States* (New York: Praeger, 1970), pp. 159–87.

10. Only one case in the McCarthy study involved a firm that received assistance, hence the conclusion is based on very limited evidence.

11. This feature of the TA apparently entered the program because of some experiences in Maine in which workers took over operations of tottering enterprises. As originally drafted in the Senate Finance Committee, employee stock ownership plans were required.

12. A relatively unknown section of the Fair Labor Standards Act (minimum wage law)—Section 4(e)—requires the secretary of labor to determine if imports are depressing wage standards in import-competing industries. Investigation is required upon request from the House, Senate, or president, or, the secretary can make an investigation on his own motion. Thus, the Labor Department did have limited monitoring responsibility even before the TA was passed. For a history of Section 4(e), see U.S., Congress, House, General Subcommittee on Labor of the Committee on Education and Labor, *Impact of Imports on American Industry and Employment Hearings held August, September, October 1966*, 89th Cong., 2d sess., 1967, pp. 3–12.

13. This proposal had been made by Labor Department officials several years before the TA was enacted. See Marvin M. Fooks, "Trade Adjustment Assistance," in Commission on International Trade and Investment Policy, *United States International Economic Policy in an Interdependent World* (Washington, D.C.: U.S. Government Printing Office, 1971), p. 363.

14. Even though the inclusion of adjustment assistance did not win the support of organized labor, it probably did help some marginal congressmen and senators vote for the TA in the face of labor opposition. One public survey indicated that favorable attitudes toward freer trade increased when people were made aware of the existence of adjustment assistance. See Charles R. Frank, Jr., *Adjustment Assistance: American Jobs and Trade with the Developing Countries* (Washington, D.C.: Overseas Development Council, 1973), p. 48.

15. A few states, such as California, have disability laws covering injury outside the workplace.

Chapter 5

1. U.S., Congress, Senate, Committee on Finance, *Implications of Multinational Firms for Trade and Investment and for U.S. Trade and Labor*, 93d Cong., 1st sess., 1973, p. 177 (study made for the committee by the Tariff Commission).

2. A study was done of the labor-intensity of multinational exports and imports in 1965. In that year, when the data given in Chapter 2 indicate the Leontief paradox was still operating for all trade, it appears that it also operated in the multinational sector. As pointed out in Chapter 2, much of the growing labor-intensity of imports after that date came via increased trade with Japan. Japan has followed a restrictive policy on foreign multinational investment in its economy, so that multinationals based in the U.S. played only a small role in this trade. See Robert E. Lipsey and Merle Yahr Weiss, "Multinational Firms and

the Factor-Intensity of Trade'' (National Bureau of Economic Research Working Paper No. 8, September 1973).

3. U.S., Congress, Senate, Committee on Finance, *Implications of Multinational Firms*, pp. 645–72.

4. Robert G. Hawkins, ''The Multinational Corporation: A New Trade Policy Issue in the United States,'' in Robert G. Hawkins and Ingo Walters, eds., *The United States and International Markets* (Lexington, Mass.: Lexington Books, 1972), p. 186.

5. Two qualifications might be noted. First, in the esoteric literature on economic ''capital theory'' it has been shown that the association of high wages and a high capital-to-labor ratio is not a theoretical necessity. Second, certain elements of international trade theory also suggest that within limits the supply of world capital could be moved from country to country without affecting real wages. See William P. Travis, *The Theory of Trade and Protection* (Cambridge, Mass.: Harvard University Press, 1964), Chapter 1; T. M. Rybczynski, ''Factor Endowment and Relative Commodity Prices,'' in Richard E. Caves and Harry G. Johnson, eds., *Readings in International Economics* (Homewood, Ill.: Richard D. Irwin, 1968), pp. 72–77.

6. It might be argued that after 1971, with the collapse of the international monetary system, the U.S. has been forced to ''pay back'' some of its debts through a devalued currency and an export surplus. This in turn has cut into domestic living standards.

7. In 1966 the reported after-tax return on assets of majority-owned foreign affiliates of U.S.-based MNCs in manufacturing averaged 4.9 percent compared to their parent firm's average of 8.1 percent. The year 1966 was an especially good one for domestic profits. In 1970 the respective figures were 5.1 percent versus 4.5 percent. See *Survey of Current Business*, May 1974, pp. 29–30.

8. Much has been written on the subject of multinational bargaining. See Daniel J. B. Mitchell, *Essays on Labor and International Trade* (Los Angeles: Institute of Industrial Relatiohs, UCLA, 1970), Chapter 4, Daniel J. B. Mitchell, ''Labor Standards and the International Coordination of Collective Bargaining,'' in Industrial Relations Research Association, *Proceedings* (December 1970), pp. 198–206; David H. Blake, ''Trade Unions and the Challenge of the Multinational Corporation,'' *Annals of the Academy of Political and Social Science* 403 (September 1972: 34–45; Herbert R. Northrup, ''Reflections on Bargaining Structure Change,'' in the Industrial Relations Research Association, *Proceedings* (December 1973), pp. 137–44.

9. John Crispo, *International Unionism: A Study of Canadian-American Relations* (Toronto: McGraw-Hill, 1967); Shirley B. Goldenberg and Frances Bairstow, eds., *Dominance or Independence? The Problem of Canadian Autonomy in Labour-Management Relations* (Montreal: Industrial Relations Centre, McGill University, 1965).

10. Herbert R. Northrup and Richard L. Rowan, ''Multinational Collective Bargaining: The Factual Record in Chemicals, Glass, and Rubber Tires,'' *Columbia Journal of World Business* 9 (Spring 1974): 112–24. The article is continued in the Summer 1974 issue, pp. 49–63.

11. Mitchell, *Essays*, pp. 69–70.

12. Ibid., pp. 75–79.

13. See U.S. Tariff Commission, *Economic Factors Affecting the Use of Items 807.00 and 806.30 of the Tariff Schedules of the United States*, TC Publication 339 (Washington, D.C.: Tariff Commission, September 1970). A position paper by the AFL–CIO is included in Appendix C.

14. Ibid., p. 19. The quote is from a report for the Senate Finance Committee prepared in 1966.

15. The impact of items 806.30 and 807.00 is not fully reflected in the calculations underlying Chapter 2. Imports coming in under these items are reported in terms of their total value, not just the assembly service which was the true import. The overall item imported may not have been especially labor-intensive, but the true service import probably was. This would have a greater impact on the 1970 figures reported in Chapter 2 than on the 1965 figures, since imports under the two items expanded relative to total imports.

16. U.S. Tariff Commission, *Economic Factors*, pp. 6–7.

17. Ibid., pp. 230–233.

18. Susumu Watanabe, "Constraints on Labour-Intensive Export Industries in Mexico," *International Labour Review* 109 (January 1974): 23–45.

19. "A Business Boomlet on Mexico's Border," *Business Week*, January 22, 1972, pp. 36–38; "Spread of U.S. Plants to Mexico Brings a Boom—And Complaints," *U.S. News and World Report*, March 27, 1972, pp. 57–59.

Library of Congress Cataloging in Publication Data

Mitchell, Daniel J   B
    Labor issues of American international trade and investment.

    (Policy studies in employment and welfare ; no. 24)
    Includes bibliographical references.

    1. Labor supply—United States. 2. United States—Commerce. I. Title.

HD5724.M6   392'.0973   76-7052
ISBN 0-8018-1848-6
ISBN 0-8018-1849-4 pbk.

112